OXFORD SHAKESPEARE TOPICS

Published and Forthcoming Titles Include:

Oxford Shakespeare Topics

GENERAL EDITORS: PETER HOLLAND AND STANLEY WELLS

Shakespeare and Marx

GABRIEL EGAN

OXFORD

UNIVERSITY PRESS

Great Clarendon Street, Oxford OX2 6DP

Oxford University Press is a department of the University of Oxford.
It furthers the University's objective of excellence in research, scholarship,
and education by publishing worldwide in

Oxford New York

Auckland Bangkok Buenos Aires Cape Town Chennai
Dar es Salaam Delhi Hong Kong Istanbul Karachi Kolkata
Kuala Lumpur Madrid Melbourne Mexico City Mumbai Nairobi
São Paulo Shanghai Taipei Tokyo Toronto

Oxford is a registered trade mark of Oxford University Press
in the UK and in certain other countries

Published in the United States
by Oxford University Press Inc., New York

© Gabriel Egan 2004

The moral rights of the author have been asserted
Database right Oxford University Press (maker)

First published 2004

British Library Cataloguing in Publication Data

Data available

Library of Congress Cataloging in Publication Data

Data available

ISBN 0-19-924993-8
ISBN 0-19-924992-x(pbk.)

10 9 8 7 6 5 4 3 2 1

Typeset by Kolam Information Services Pvt. Ltd, Pondicherry, India
Printed in Great Britain
on acid-free paper by
Biddles Ltd,
King's Lynn, Norfolk

Acknowledgements

I thank Nigel Wood for a lunch (probably forgotten) during which he casually explained how to start this book and Kiernan Ryan for stopping me when, despite the best efforts of friends and colleagues, it went in the wrong direction. I was guided by expert editorial commentary from the series general editors Peter Holland and Stanley Wells and from Frances Whistler and Elizabeth Prochaska at the press. The usefulness of the Shakespeare Institute's library in Stratford-on-Avon is immeasurably increased by the specialist knowledge of its custodians James Shaw and Kate Welch, to whom I have long been a debtor. John W. Kennedy provided information about David Heneker's song 'The Thing-ummy-bob' and Nigel Wood an anecdote about *Waiting for Godot* used in Chapter 2. John Jowett gave advance notice of his work on Thomas Middleton's input to *Timon of Athens* used in Chapter 4.

Here it is customary to give thanks to funding bodies for research grants and to employers for sabbatical leave that helped the work along. Writing this book as an employee of Shakespeare's Globe Theatre between 2001 and 2003 I had neither, but I would like to thank the staff of Chiltern Railways, especially those at Warwick Parkway station, whose unfailingly cheerful efficiency made it a pleasure to write this book aboard their Birmingham to London service between 2001 and 2003. My return journey was rarely delayed and always sweetened by anticipation of the companionship of my wife, Joan Fitzpatrick.

This book is dedicated to my brother Paschal Egan, in appreciation of early lessons in the indivisibility of Marxism and humour.

Contents

A Note on References

References are given by parenthetical author and date, followed by page numbers where relevant, keyed to the single list of works given on pp. 153–62. Unless otherwise stated, all quotations of Shakespeare are from the *Oxford Complete Works* edited by Stanley Wells and Gary Taylor (Shakespeare 1986). Other quotations from writers of Shakespeare's time are from recent, modernized texts or else I have silently modernized the quotations. Where a year alone appears in brackets after a book's title, this is the year of first publication and is given to evoke the historical context in which the work appeared, although quotations may well be drawn from a subsequent edition cited, as always, by author-date.

A Note on Dates and Pronouns

One of this book's themes is the fact that everyday language embodies particular ways of understanding the world, and a couple of notable examples bear upon my own practice. Most of the world reckons its dates in relation to the birth of Jesus Christ, from which we count backward (BC = before Christ) and forward (AD = *Anno Domini*, Latin for 'in the year of our Lord'). In recognition of the fact that many people do not consider Jesus Christ to be their 'Lord', historians have settled upon a pair of labels that I will use: BCE (before Common Era, equivalent to BC) and CE (Common Era, equivalent to AD). In the same spirit, I avoid the use of the masculine pronouns 'he' and 'his' where gender is unimportant to the sense. English is notably deficient in gender-neutral pronouns, and since many years of conventional usage have established that one of the genders may stand for both, I have elected to use 'she' and 'her' in this way.

Marxist thinking about culture underlies much research and teaching in university departments of literature and played a crucial role in the development of recent theoretical work. Feminism, New Historicism, cultural materialism, postcolonial theory, and queer theory all draw upon ideas about cultural production that can be traced to Marx, and significantly each also has a special relation with Renaissance literary studies. Despite this, Marx's main ideas are seldom properly explained in works about Shakespeare and in some quarters it is even claimed that they have lost their relevance. This book aims to explain the past and present influence of Marxism for Shakespearians, and to suggest ways in which it can play a role in the future of politically engaged literary and dramatic criticism and cultural analysis.

Concern for oppressed people was one of Marx's enduring legacies to twentieth-century thinking about politics and literature, although Marx frequently represented his ideas as scientific discoveries rather than components of a political morality. For Marx, capitalism was doomed to a finite lifespan because of its inherent limitations, not merely because it was unfair. For students of literature Marx's most important work is on the relationship between creativity and economic production, leading to the assertion that 'consciousness arises out of social being'. Marx's model of a society's base (the way production is organized) and superstructure (the corresponding mental systems including jurisprudence, education, and art) looks like reductive determinism if the superstructure is thought to merely serve the needs of the base. Marx repeatedly stressed that thinking escapes the confines of material circumstances and the essence of his determinism was the notion that language, a social construct, shapes consciousness as well as being an expression of it. As we shall see in Chapter 1 and the Conclusion, linguistics went on to bolster this constructivist view in ways that conflict with recent science.

For Marx, social being and consciousness were not to be considered as static but rather as mutually self-sustaining in their progression, whilst at the same time mutually conditioned by one another. Attempts to improve upon Marx's model of base and superstructure have not entirely removed the objection that the model, howsoever nuanced, is inherently reductive. One stumbling block is the multiplicity of meanings in which Marx used the notion of ideology, which remains the superstructural entity or process (it is not clear which it is) of prime interest. As we shall see in Chapter I, Marx's definition of ideology occasionally seems slightly confused and he refined it several times to remove certain contradictions that became apparent.

My survey of Marx's influence will pick out figures of particular importance for their work on Shakespeare, starting with George Bernard Shaw, as well as tracing the development of Marx's ideas by others after his death. Noting that Shakespeare's working class characters are generally unpleasant, Shaw explained this as observation, not political sentiment, and asserted that no one could have thought otherwise in Shakespeare's time. Arguing *ad hominem*, and treating the Elizabethan mind-set as essentially closed to ideas whose time had not come, Shaw displayed a limited grasp of Marx's sense of the relationship between art and economic production. The workers, for Shaw, were other people whose minds were retarded by the effects of their oppression.

Bertolt Brecht took almost precisely the opposite view and his ideas about theatre were the first major dramatic expression of Marx's ideas about ideology and can be paralleled with the Russian Formalists' interest in literature as writing that disturbs everyday habits of thought. Brecht saw the conventions of representations as themselves superstructural and at least partially oriented to the needs of the current economic system. Original Elizabethan performance conditions had, for Brecht, a useful awkwardness that made apparent the means of representation, and he valued Shakespeare's sense of contradiction, his capturing of the dialectic of existence. Refusing to allow endings to resolve contradictions, Brecht championed the Marxist dialectic of endless self-contradiction.

Marxist thinking entered mainstream Shakespeare studies in the 1980s via the British Cultural Materialism and American New Historicism. The Cultural Materialists made much of their rejection of E. M. W. Tillyard's rigid model of Elizabethan attitudes towards order, hierarchy, social stasis, and historical progress. In attempting to codify what a typical educated Elizabethan might think and feel about key social and political issues, Tillyard effectively mapped what Marxists mean by ideology, and the strongly negative reaction to Tillyardism in the 1980s was a disagreement about what exactly that Elizabethan ideology consisted of—especially regarding the space for unorthodox ideas—rather than a rejection of the general principle that one might indeed be able to map it. In essence, Tillyard was guilty of a vulgar kind of Marxism, although by re-examination of his *The Elizabethan World Picture* (1943) I will show that it was less vulgar than has been claimed.

The emancipatory struggles of the 1960s were initiated by raised consciousness concerning racial, sexual, and (in Northern Ireland especially) religious discrimination. In the 1960s and 1970s historicism gained a new range of subject positions from which to perceive the past, and working-class history, women's history, and the history of oppressed races became legitimate studies. Criticism concerned with sexual orientation continues the trend begun by gender and race criticism in the 1970s. Recently, postcolonial theory has become less concerned with international expansion and more concerned with the complexities of subject-definition: how does a colonizer identify a native as 'other'? The Marxist idea that categories of difference are not immanent but rather are historically contingent has led to the popular assertion that homosexuality itself was not a subject position (as we might say, an identity) but a practice.

Drawing upon the ideas examined in the first three chapters, I give readings of seven plays: *The Merchant of Venice*, *Timon of Athens*, *King Lear*, *Hamlet*, *All's Well That Ends Well*, *The Comedy of Errors*, and *The Winter's Tale*. The first two directly concern individuals' relations with money, but in all the potentially deterministic relationship between material reality and the world of ideas is important. The economic imperatives at work in *The Merchant of Venice* can be understood as a tension between pre-capitalist and capitalist notions of the correct uses of money, and one that was heightened by the contemporary experience of price inflation, which made hoarding a sure way to lose it. Marxist principles of economic class antagonism throw light on Shylock's impeccable defence of his right to own Antonio's flesh, since the Venetian state upholds the principle of slavery. Shylock invokes an ancient ideological construct (the ownership of human flesh) that capitalism disavowed in replacing the market in human flesh with a market in its derivative, labour. In *The Merchant of Venice* and *Timon of Athens*, different ways of making use of money are explored in relation to reciprocal bonds of social interaction.

The reading of *King Lear* offered here focuses on the play's exploration of the possibilities for future change. In one version of the play, the Fool makes a prophecy about 'Albion' that editors since the eighteenth century have altered in ways that suggest their views on utopianism. One of Marx's most influential inheritors in the late twentieth century was the French philosopher Jacques Derrida, and the reading of *Hamlet* offered here critiques his work on the limitations of representations (such as the play-within-the-play) as means to get at the truth.

All's Well That Ends Well marks a significant deviation from Shakespeare's usual depiction of war in that the causes of the Florentine/Sienese conflict are of no interest to the young noblemen of France who fight on either side in it. The play can be read as a criticism of the pursuit of war for 'breathing and exploit' by an aristocratic class whose military *raison d'être* has disappeared. In its place they have a shocking indifference to human individuality, and this is at the heart of the lesson Helen teaches Bertram.

My reading of *The Comedy of Errors* focuses on subjectivity—how we know who we are—from a Marxist perspective that insists that our sense of ourselves depends on our relations with others. In Ephesus the boys from Syracuse find themselves already known and treated as old acquaintances in a city that is entirely new to them, and the play repeatedly uses mirroring (of the twins, of husband and wife, and of a prostitute's clients) to represent the principle of exchangeability that underlies what Marx called commodity fetishism. Finally, I will argue that in *The Winter's Tale* Shakespeare tackled the topical matter of social mobility and found a way to reconcile the rising power of the bourgeoisie with an essentially conservative political outlook.

In the Conclusion I return to the dilemmas of the base/superstructure model of determination and liken them to a persistent dilemma in the physical sciences concerning genetic and environmental determination. It is widely but incorrectly believed in social sciences that neo-Darwinism deterministically attributes primary influence over human behaviour to genetic forces and subordinates culture to nature. In fact, genetics illustrates the same self-reflexivity that Marxists have long fretted about in their own sphere, for without the necessary environment for DNA to be copied these tiny slivers of matter cannot make the 'machines' (living creatures) that replicate them.

Behaviour and environment are already built into the processes that genes operate within and rather than utterly shaping behaviour, genes have evolved in relation to an environment that, to a great extent, consists of the expressed behaviour coded by other genes. As an extension of genetics, the new and hotly contested discipline of memetics is the study of the spread and evolution of ideas and concepts (e.g. jokes, catchphrases, political ideas) in a collective of human minds. Memetics provides a materialist way of thinking about the relationship between ideas and reality. In the subtle and complex relationship between genetic and memetic imperatives, language and literature flourish as mental phenomena that interpenetrate personal and social existence and offer powerful means for the rational reorganization of both.

1

Shakespeare, Marx, Production, and the World of Ideas

In Act 2, Scene 2 of David Edgar's play *The Prisoner's Dilemma* (first performed 2001) Tom Rothman, an American academic, likens recent inter-ethnic conflict in eastern Europe to 'those scenes in Shakespeare plays where guys called towns turn out to be first cousins married to each other's sisters' (Edgar 2001, 103). The parallel is not frivolous: the disintegration of one pole of the binarily opposed armed camps of the Cold War released latent tensions about ethnicity and nationhood that *are* like the murderous energies released by the epochal shifts dramatized in Shakespeare's history plays. But as a joke, Rothman's comment is illuminating.

The names of Shakespeare's aristocrats are confusing, and sometimes they seem to relish the confusion. In the trial-by-combat in *Richard II*, the man whose speech prefix is Bolingbroke at the start of the play (he will end it as King Henry) answers the question 'Who are you?' with a list of places: 'Harry of Hereford, Lancaster, and Derby' (1.3.35–6). This 'of' means that he is not merely from these places but rules them. Bolingbroke is the son of John of Gaunt (who is Duke of Lancaster), a man with two names: the first denoting where he comes from (Ghent) and the second where he rules. (Historically, no one called him John of Gaunt after he was three years old, until Shakespeare's play popularized this form of his name.) About the middle of the play Bolingbroke returns from banishment to claim his inheritance, which enrages his uncle the Duke of York. Bolingbroke's response sounds like quibbling,

'As I was banished, I was banished Hereford; / But as I come, I come for Lancaster' (2.3.112–13), but he sticks to his claim that his change of name embodies his right to be Duke of Lancaster after his father:

> BERKELEY
> My lord of Hereford, my message is to you.
> BOLINGBROKE
> My lord, my answer is to 'Lancaster',
> And I am come to seek that name in England,
> And I must find that title in your tongue
> Before I make reply to aught you say.
>
> (2.3.69–73)

This is no mere matter of polite address, for with Bolingbroke's change of name comes a change in who he is. Insistence upon the point illustrates his claim that either rights of succession are inalienable or they are not: if the king's right to inherit from *his* father is absolute, says Bolingbroke, then so is mine.

Under Henry's rule as king of England in the second half of the play, other names change too:

> DUCHESS OF YORK
> Here comes my son Aumerle.
> YORK   Aumerle that was;
> But that is lost for being Richard's friend,
> And, madam, you must call him 'Rutland' now.
>
> (5.2.41–3)

Aumerle's complicity in a plot against the new king divides his parents, the Duchess of York wanting to preserve her only son and the Duke cravenly seeking to denounce him in order to demonstrate loyalty to the new ruler. Although the speech prefixes for Henry Bolingbroke, Duke of Hereford (and later Lancaster), change midway through the play to 'King Henry', most play-text editions leave Aumerle as Aumerle even after he is supposed to be Rutland. Such things bother and confuse readers more than spectators in a theatre, because speech prefixes are not spoken aloud; in performance characters just are whatever others call them and we recognize them by identifying the actors. However, the Duchess of York uses her son's new name, in the act of pleading for his life:

KING HENRY
  Rise up, good aunt.
DUCHESS OF YORK   Not yet, I thee beseech.
  Forever will I kneel upon my knees,
  And never see day that the happy sees,
  Till thou give joy, until thou bid me joy
  By pardoning Rutland, my transgressing boy.

                        (5.3.90–4)

We might say that she is merely conforming to the king's nomenclature to strengthen her appeal for mercy—who is not flattered to hear their names for things being taken up by others?—but in this play the matter of how things and people are named is a central concern because it dramatizes a remarkable rupture in the English monarchy. Richard II was quite simply the last medieval king to rule in England by hereditary right, and so it is no surprise that the man who usurps him renames himself and those around him, for his project is nothing less than a wholesale redefinition of the relationships at the top of the English aristocracy.

Real life, including such fundamental political change, might seem far from the abstract world of ideas, but obviously the two cannot entirely be disconnected. Social changes are made by people with ideas, clearly, but what of the reciprocal relationship? How far are ideas themselves shaped by how life is lived? Two extremist views are identifiable: the ultra-Idealists who hold that human beings are free to think anything without constraint and the ultra-Materialists who insist that all thought is causally dependent upon physical processes. Marx has long been thought to be near the ultra-Materialist end of the spectrum because he reduces everything, including the ideas one might be able to think, to economic processes that his theories explain. Worse still, Marxism has been characterized as a set of political doctrines that actually tell people what to think and punishes those whose ideas are not 'politically correct'. To see how wrong this is, we must look to Marx's philosophical studies and their contribution to materialism.

   In April 1841 Marx, then 32, received his doctorate from the University of Jena for a thesis called 'The Difference between the Democritean and the Epicurean Philosophy of Nature'. Through the 1840s Marx turned from ancient philosophy to modern philosophy and political economy and around the end of 1844 he made a decisive shift away from what he later came to think of as superstructure—philosophy, jurisprudence, morals, and ideology—in order to focus on the real basis of all human activity: the underlying economic structure. In the preface to *A Contribution to the Critique of Political Economy* (1859), Marx explained his move from philosophy to economic matters as a consequence of becoming editor of the journal *Rheinische Zeitung*, in which some practical matters came up for debate. To satisfy his own interests in these he undertook a critical review of Georg Hegel's philosophy of law and found that law and legal relations, including the forms of the state, are rooted in the material conditions of life. The general, and now much-quoted, conclusion that Marx reached was this:

> In the social production of their existence, men inevitably enter into definite relations, which are independent of their will, namely relations of production appropriate to a given stage in the development of their material forces of production. The totality of these relations of production constitutes the economic structure of society, the real foundation, on which rises a legal and political superstructure and to which correspond definite forms of social consciousness. The mode of production of material life conditions the general process of social, political and intellectual life. It is not the consciousness of men that determines their existence, but their social existence that determines their consciousness. (Marx 1970, 20–1)

The claim that social existence (or social being, as it is sometimes translated) determines consciousness has become a central tenet of Marxism but its precise meaning is endlessly debated. In particular, what kind of influence does Marx mean by 'determine' and what aspects of life are one's 'social being'? Most sympathetic readers seek ways to understand the superstructure or the individual consciousness as generally shaped but not entirely constrained by economics. After all, the reader who grasps this idea is, surely, already thinking outside the narrow limits of economics. Much of the present book will be concerned with this dilemma and its implications for the study of artistic writing, especially by Shakespeare, since of all the fruits of consciousness, literature seems least fettered.

What might Henry Bolingbroke's 'social being' be? It might mean his place in the world around him, as a senior aristocrat and leader of a familial dynasty (the Lancastrians) in political dispute with other families, as a man amongst late-medieval warriors whose legitimacy as rulers was at least partly predicated on their ability to fight using the technology and martial theory of the day, and, at the start of *Richard II*, as an exiled victim of another's conspiracies. According to Marx, these aspects of his 'social being' make him what he is, not only in the sense of providing the context for his actions, offering opportunities (such as fighting to prove one's innocence) and constraints (if the king banishes you, you go), but also forming his consciousness. In other words, his sense of who he is, his own reflection upon his situation, and the mind that does that reflecting (as well as the self it reflects upon) are all created by his place in the world. His consciousness, then, is different from that of the groom of the stable who comforts Richard in prison because they have entirely different places in the world.

This does not seem a controversial assertion, yet Marx's statement that 'consciousness arises out of social being' has been widely taken as a deeply pessimistic and mechanically deterministic view of the human mind. After all, if we are only the sum of our social circumstances there seems little chance to celebrate individual human achievements of the mind: the great mathematicians or musicians were bound to produce what they did, since they experienced the conditions that gave rise to them. Obviously, no one really believes that the relationship between circumstances and consciousness is so mechanical, but perhaps surprisingly throughout Shakespeare studies people have written as though they believe it. As we shall see (pp. 62–8 below), E. M. W. Tillyard's model of what he called the 'Elizabethan World Picture' came close to such a mechanism, and a major branch of British Shakespeare studies has grown out of rejecting Tillyardism. On the other hand, American New Historicism began with a book whose promising title of *Renaissance Self-Fashioning* (1980) doubly suggested that it would be about a person's ability to freely fashion his or her self as well as the way that the self is fashioned by impersonal forces. However, towards the end, its author Stephen Greenblatt declared that he began with an optimism that the former would be paramount but as the work progressed he found that examples of the latter dominated.

In tracing a history of Marx's place in twentieth-century Shakespeare studies, this book will attempt to identify the deadening hand of mechanistic views of human creativity whether coming from the political left or right. My conviction is that Marx's view of determination is optimistic and liberating and that it has been misapplied (where it has not simply been misunderstood), with effects quite contrary to Marx's intentions. To see how that has happened requires first an outline explanation of Marx's ideas about the relationship between economics, all kinds of production (practical and artistic), and historical change.

Marx on Production and History

Starting as I did with an aristocratic character is not how Marx would have begun to explain his ideas, for his primary concern was the great mass of oppressed workers in the Europe of the mid-nineteenth century. Marx's ideas about production began with this reality all around him, for he believed that these people would be the engine of great historical change, throwing off their oppression and creating a world run for the benefit of all rather than a few. Marx first applied his philosophical training to a consideration of how a worker feels about her work under the prevailing conditions. Previous writings on political economy always assumed the existence of private property as a given, as though it were as natural as the land or sea, whereas for Marx the existence of private property was part of what economic theory must account for. (This was to become a recurring interpretative move in Marxism: take a step back from a socially accepted given and show it to be contingent, not immanent.)

The more a worker works, Marx observed, the poorer she becomes and inevitably the objects she makes but cannot afford to own seem alien to her and she feels dominated by them. The assertion that workers get poorer the more they work seems odd to us, but Marx lived in a period of virtually unregulated exploitation with little state control over working hours, child labour, and safety standards, and for the most part conditions were getting worse. Moreover, in Marx's mind the proper comparison was between these conditions and those that had preceded them under late feudalism. From that point of view, the condition of the working class was a desperate descent into misery. Before capitalism, the makers of products had owned the things necessary for production, such as sheep and spinning wheels, or seeds and hoes, in Marx's terms the 'means of production'. The essence of capitalism is that the makers of things do not possess their own means of production: they have the skill and knowledge to make, but cannot do it because they have no tools or raw materials. Capitalism happens when such potential workers, possessing only their own labouring power, meet people who have the tools and raw materials; at such a meeting the owners of the means of production are at an advantage and can set the terms of the transaction.

Building on the work of the bourgeois economists Adam Smith and David Ricardo, Marx adopted the 'labour theory of value', which asserts that human labour alone imbues objects with value. What does it mean to say that a certain pair of shoes is worth £40 and a certain piano is worth £400? There are few things that can be done with a piano that can also be done with shoes, let alone done ten times better. Pianos and shoes are incommensurable, yet one can exchange these items. On the open market a trader will in all likelihood accept ten pairs of such shoes for the piano, and another would accept the opposite exchange. In many markets one is not taken seriously unless one has vast quantities to exchange, but the principle is the same: a million barrels of crude oil can easily be exchanged for seven thousand tons of tin if one knows the right people in London, New York, or Tokyo. Marx argued that there must be some third quantity x, apart from shoes and pianos or oil and tin, of which the shoes have $1x$, and a piano has $10x$. This third quantity is not money, since the exchange principle works equally well in economies that use only barter. Marx decided that this mysterious third quantity was labour, the concentrated human effort that went into making the thing.

The assertion that labour is the underlying essence of all value in human society is a philosophical proposition that many find attractive, but for Marx it was also a truth like the law of gravity, and it would have consequences at least as important as Isaac Newton's discovery. Where Newton's principle linked all places—the planets circling the sun obey the same laws as a child's spinning top—Marx's labour theory of value linked all productive civilizations from our earliest tool-making ancestors to the sweatshops of Victorian England and beyond to the coming workers' paradise.

The transaction between a worker and an employer is based on the former selling her labour to the latter, and on terms that are unfavourable to the worker who nonetheless accepts them because she has no other way to produce anything to keep herself alive. A simple way to state the terms of the transaction is that the worker receives less for her work than the value she adds to the employer's goods she works upon, so that if by her work she turns £100 of raw materials into something worth £200, she is paid £50 and the other £50 is the employer's profit. This is how the transaction is commonly explained, but Marx wanted his economic theory to be founded on firm principles about exact amounts of value changing hands and needed to avoid the suggestion that if only a reasonable wage could be found capitalism might be made fair. He decided that workers do not directly sell their labour at all; rather what they sell is their labour power for an agreed and limited time. Were the duration unlimited, a lifetime, then the worker would be the employer's slave rather than employee. Time is built into the arrangements between employers and employees and so it is worked into the articles made. Since labour is the sole source of value, it is absurdly circular to ask 'What is the value of labour?' because the value of 10 hours labour is precisely 10 hours labour. We can ask a slightly different question, however: 'What is the value of labouring power?' That is to say, we can treat the ability to labour as a made article produced by the birth, raising, and maintenance of the labourer.

Like everything else, the value of this made article is the quantity of labour that went into making it: the work done in giving birth to it, raising it, and keeping it from day to day. The quantity of labour necessary to produce a labourer is whatever she consumes to stay alive plus whatever it takes to raise a child to take her place when she wears out. (Notice again the stepping back and making a given into something contingent.) Of course, not all labouring powers are of the same value. According to Marx, equality of wages is an absurd idea if what matters is 'the value of the necessaries required to produce, develop, maintain, and perpetuate the labouring power' (Marx 1899, 58); it clearly takes more of those necessaries to produce a brain surgeon than a roadsweeper.

Suppose that to keep a labourer for a day—that is, to produce what the labourer consumes in a day—requires 5 hours of average labour, which is also the number of hours necessary to produce gold to the value of £100. The price and the value of the labourer's daily labouring power would be £100, and if she worked 5 hours a day she would produce a value exactly equivalent to the amount needed to maintain herself, and that value would be transferred to whatever she made.

However, by buying the daily value of the labouring power of the worker, the capitalist has the right to use her for more than the 5 hours needed to replace her wages, and if she works another 5 hours as well this surplus labour will generate surplus value transferred to whatever she makes. For every £100 put out in wages (what it takes to sustain a labourer for a day), the capitalist gets £200 value.

The labourer naturally, but wrongly, assumes that her labour for the whole day is worth what the capitalist gives her, but in fact she is given only the amount needed to maintain herself to be able to come back tomorrow and do it again. The labourer does not realize that she earned that value long before her day was done. So although it seems that she was paid for the whole day, really the first part of the day was paid labour (up to the point where she had worked to the value of the necessaries of a day's survival) and the rest of the day was unpaid labour.

It is worth comparing this situation to its two main historical antecedents: the slave feels herself to be working unpaid all the time (although in reality the first part of the day is spent producing the value she consumes in food given her by the slave-owner), and the serf alone gets to see the difference between the paid labour (time spent on land growing crops that feed the serf's family) and unpaid labour (time spent on the land growing crops kept by the landowner). In our example, an average hour of labour generates £20 (so 10 hours = £200) and the value of a day's labour (the amount needed to sustain a labourer) is £100, the product of five hours of labour. Suppose that a heap of raw material for a commodity has the value of 20 hours labour, or in other words £400. Say the worker adds 10 hours labour (worth £200) to the heap of raw material making its value now £600. The capitalist gives the worker her daily wage of £100, so no one has paid for the other 5 hours (worth £100) value added to the commodity. It is this profit of £100 that the capitalist reaps when selling the article for £600. The thing is sold *at its real value*, not an inflated one, and thus yields a profit: the capitalist put out £400 on materials, £100 on labour, and got back £600 for this £500. The employing capitalist might have to give some of the profit to a landlord (in rent) or moneylender (in interest), but the surplus value did not come from the land or the capital but from the unpaid labour of the worker. It is not the case that profit (or indeed rent or interest repayment) is added to a commodity to compute its final value, rather unpaid-for value is put in by the labourer and the capitalist takes from this value the profit, perhaps losing some to rent and interest repayment.

Marx expressed these economic views in a talk of 1865 (Marx 1899, 41–94), and they appeared in print in 1867 in the first volume of *Capital*. The remaining volumes of *Capital* were not completed by Marx, but from his notes and drafts Frederick Engels produced volumes two and three and Karl Kautsky produced volume four. There are obvious objections to Marx's 'labour theory of value' that we should deal with right away. Surely if value depends on labouring time, one reaches the absurd conclusion that things become more valuable if the worker is lazy and takes longer than necessary to make it? To avoid this, Marx made a distinction between 'concrete' labour (how long it actually took) and 'socially necessary' labour (how long it should have taken). The amount of necessary labour depends on conditions such as the machines available, the skill of the labourer, and the ease of getting the materials. When a new machine becomes available that speeds up production this lowers the amount of necessary labour to make a thing, so those who do not have the machine will have to work more of their inefficient 'concrete' hours to generate the same value as one of the 'necessary' hours using the machine. If things become harder to make—as with food if less fertile soil is used—then more labour is being put into them and hence their value rises; conversely, if things become easier to make—say yarn, because a spinning machine has been bought—then less labour goes into each metre and its value falls. Thus the general prevailing conditions such as the fertility of land, the wealth of mines, the quality of transport systems, and the concentrations of capital in machines provide a context in which a collectively agreed amount of labour is needed to make any particular product.

The natural price of a made article, Marx understood from Adam Smith, is the amount of labour congealed in it, and this will vary from one individual sample to the next since some will have been made in different conditions of production from others. However, there is also the market price, which is the same for all articles of the same kind and is simply the average amount of social labour necessary, given the average conditions, to make the article. If one were to take a long view that evens out local distortions, one would see that market prices fluctuate around, and are gravitating towards, their respective natural prices, which is the same as their true values. Marx accepted that things might temporarily sell at prices higher than their real values, but he pointed out that this cannot last long because every capitalist's attempt to make a profit by selling would be frustrated by the inflated price to be paid for the raw materials.

Importantly, Marx's view of what happens in capitalism is counter-intuitive, and readers who are not convinced about the difference between 'concrete' and 'socially necessary' labour time might consult John Weeks's *Capital and Exploitation* (Weeks 1981, 27–49), which shows that once labouring power is traded in a market—a defining characteristic of the capitalist system—those who miscalculate how much time is necessary to make something are beaten in competition by those who get it right, and thus 'socially necessary' labour time emerges as an ideal governing the actions of capitalists.

Marx's concern has a double focus, on the individual labourer being exploited, about which he clearly felt pity and anger, and on the large historical picture of a succession of epochs distinguished by the dominant mode of production (slavery, feudalism, capitalism, and socialism). A Marxist approach to Shakespeare could attend to either of these two foci, the former by looking for individual working-class characters in the plays and analysing their particular situation, and the latter by considering how Shakespeare depicts epochal change, as in the differences between the newly formed republic of fifth-century BCE Rome depicted in *Coriolanus*, or the first-century CE transition from republic to monarchy depicted in *Julius Caesar*, or the eclectic setting of *Titus Andronicus* that 'collapses the whole of Roman history' in order to interrogate 'what kind of an example it provides for Elizabethan England' (Shakespeare 1995, 17).

In isolation these are valuable activities, but the genius of Marx is how he relates the individual to historical change and insists that, working together, individuals make their own history even though the conditions under which they make it are not of their choosing. Shakespeare too is concerned with historical changes, and many of his plays depict how large effects result from the actions of individuals. One way to relate the two is the idea of ripeness, that systems of government reach a cusp at which point a relatively small intervention by the right person at the right time tips them over into a wholly new state, as expressed by Brutus:

> There is a tide in the affairs of men
> Which, taken at the flood, leads on to fortune;
> Omitted, all the voyage of their life
> Is bound in shallows and in miseries.
>
> (*Julius Caesar*, 4.2.270–3)

The moment in men's lives corresponds to a moment in the wider world, so that seizing it has large historical consequences. This active principle is a useful corrective to the pessimistic Marxism of some studies that place all the emphasis on the impersonal forces that shape individuals, so that for example in the literary-critical school of British Cultural Materialism (discussed in detail in Chapter 3) the concern is often with the ways that individuals are powerless in the face of societal forces that oppress them.

Bertolt Brecht used a different Marxist approach again, showing that the (albeit prescribed) choices made by minor characters are rational ones that we might make in the same situation. Thus in the tavern scenes in the Henry IV plays, Brecht would dress the stage so that staying indoors by a warm fire with good company, food, and drink was infinitely more sensible than braving the dangers of travelling at night or fighting a battle. Rather than align himself with the traditional interpretation of the plays—that feminized cowardly low characters will do anything to avoid the trials of manly martial action—Brecht sought a staging that provided a visual correlative to the low characters' choices. It is entirely possible that the original productions did this also, or at least provided grounds for conflictual feelings in the original audiences, and that modern productions mistake the play in representing the world that Prince Hal gives up as merely an adolescent indulgence.

Ideas and the Base/Superstructure Model

In a Marxist view economics is the underlying force that gives shape to everything else, even consciousness. How far should we take this claim literally in everyday life? I certainly feel entirely free to have my next thought and write my next sentence any way I choose, but this freedom must be to some degree delusional, for if I choose to now abandon my argument about Marx and Shakespeare and devote the remainder of this chapter to the superiority of Italian ice cream over the Cornish variety, agents in the power structure of academic publishing (specifically, the general editors of this series and their commissioning editor at Oxford University Press) will almost certainly not print it. I have a set of instructions for how this book should develop, and others working on behalf of the press have the power to cancel my contract if I fail to meet their brief, which event would have economic consequences for my future as a worker within higher education. That this does not feel like coercion is not because the economic power relations are not really there—indisputably they are—but because my reaching this stage of the work has only been possible because of an ongoing, albeit approximate, alignment of various interests: of the press, of its commissioning editor (who persuaded the press that the Oxford Shakespeare Topics series was a desirable project), of the general editors (who persuaded the commissioning editor that the series should contain a volume on Shakespeare and Marx), and finally of me who persuaded the general editors and the press that I was the person to write it. Arguably, the freedom of individual thought is still preserved in all this, since a major publisher in the capitalist marketplace is paying for a book that, by aiming to persuade its readers that Marx was right, seeks to undermine the economic system upon which it rests; this is a contradiction to which I will return.

Economic forces obviously underlie every human activity, since one cannot begin a productive working day (whether labouring, writing, raising children, or contemplatively thinking) without food and lodging. However, Marx's understanding of how economics underlies everything goes deeper than these practicalities because his model of the superstructure arising from the economic base includes the most basic institutions, practices, and habits of mind: 'the general process of social, political and intellectual life' (Marx 1970, 20–1).

It is clear how a writer might be constrained by economics—if the book seems unlikely to sell, it probably will not reach the market—but surely that is a special case. It is harder to see how economics might determine the intellectual life of someone working in a hospital doing things apparently shaped only by the needs of the human body, such as mending broken limbs and emptying bedpans. One way it might happen is through language, theories of which were hotly contested throughout the twentieth century. A pragmatic approach to language would treat words as merely convenient tags for objects in the real world, created so that in the absence of the things themselves their spoken representatives might be employed. This necessity is avoided by the Balnibarbians of Jonathan Swift's *Gulliver's Travels* (1726), who carry on their backs all the objects about which they might need to converse, and communicate by holding these out to one another in exchanges of mute display (Swift 1985, 230). In the preface to his dictionary of 1755, Samuel Johnson gave the same pragmatic view of language as a labelling system—'Language is only the instrument of science, and words are but the signs of ideas' (Johnson 1773, iv)—and the persistence of this view in the nineteenth century is attested by the decision of James Murray that, unless otherwise stated, words in the *New English Dictionary on Historical Principles* (1884–1928), later re-named the *Oxford English Dictionary*, could be assumed to be nouns (Simpson and Weiner 1989, xxvii). For Marx, however, language was not principally about things but about people:

Language is as old as consciousness, language *is* practical consciousness that exists also for other men, and for that reason alone it really exists for me as well; language, like consciousness, arises only from the need, the necessity, of intercourse with other men. (Marx and Engels 1974, 51)

The idea that language is not about our relationships with things but rather our relationships with each other was to be a powerful one in the twentieth century, starting with the linguistics that Ferdinand de Saussure taught in Geneva before the First World War (Saussure 1960). Saussure was concerned with the rules that govern utterance and observed that a competent speaker of a language can detect and correct errors in an ungrammatical utterance even if unable to state the rules explicitly. The internalized rules common to all competent speakers of a language Saussure called a *langue* and a particular utterance conforming to them he called a *parole*.

Saussure's theory about what happens when we hear someone speaking has been enormously influential in literary studies, although alarmingly the professional linguists abandoned it in the 1950s and, as I shall argue in my conclusion, literature specialists should follow them. When we speak, Saussure claimed, we make sounds that cause other people who are listening to have mental images appear in their heads without any effort. If someone says 'cat', you have no choice about the matter: the idea of a four-legged furry animal arises in your head. This works because as speakers of English we have agreed upon a sign composed of two parts: the signifier is the sound made with the throat and mouth, and the signified is the mental image that pops into your head. A signifier can be altered quite considerably without creating confusion, so that by changing the vowel sound 'a' in 'cat' one might produce a spoken sound close to what standard English represents as 'kite' or 'cart', but if the context is sufficiently strong (such as 'I took my cat to the vet') the listener will still experience the feline signified.

Language, Saussure decided, operates by unconscious mental negation that automatically excludes the wrong choices to arrive at the right one, and for many sounds there are no nearby ones that could suggest a new, wrong, signified. Deforming the vowel sound in 'vat' to make 'vite' or 'vart' does not direct the hearer to a new signified because unlike 'cat', the sign 'vat' does not have close neighbours with these sounds. This seemingly uncontroversial idea has wide-ranging consequences that will become clear when we consider how the distribution of signifiers might vary in a foreign language. When someone says the English word 'beef' we know they mean the meat of a dead cow because there is another word, 'cow', to signify the living animal. In French, however, the word 'boeuf' can mean a live cow or its flesh when dead. These choices are not derived from hard reality but social convention, just as the colours of the rainbow are in many cultures divided into bands of red, orange, yellow, green, blue, indigo, and violet even though in physics this reality is not a matter of categories but smoothly increasing frequency of the light. Language divides the smooth continuum into seven bands, and in other languages the divisions have been made elsewhere: some people see nine or more narrower bands, others see four or five wider ones. An example used by Terence Hawkes is the Welsh word 'glas' that corresponds to the English words 'blue' and 'green' (Hawkes 2002, 24). (As I shall show in my conclusion, there are severe problems with such arguments based on Saussure.) The structuring of experience is a facility of the human mind, and we do it without trying.

If we accept Saussure's model of language operating by sequences of negation and distinction we are on the way to admitting that, in an important sense, language is constitutive of reality and not merely a set of tags for it, that the things that our minds discriminate between are not 'out there' in the world but inside our heads, and the categories are placed there by the culture in which we grow up. The French using a single signifier, 'boeuf', for live and dead cows does not prevent them making the distinction (indeed they also have the word 'vache' to mean just the living animal), and it gives them the freedom to make an ironical inversion not available in English. A French animal rights activist working in a restaurant might lead a living cow to my table and utter a contemptuous 'Voici votre boeuf!', which would be literally true although I actually wanted a steak. The rhetorical force of this act would be lost in English, since 'Here is your beef' would not be true, so the available language determines someone's power to confront me with the agricultural reality underlying my eating habits. For much of what we say there can be no such thing as mere translation: the only way to turn the French waiter's comment into English with the same rhetorical force is to find an entirely different form of words exploiting an analogous ambiguity in the English language.

Political engagements such as the animal rights movement are for many people an important part of reality and clearly that reality has already been conditioned linguistically before it is encountered politically. Although the number of examples has been distorted by the compilers of the *Oxford English Dictionary* having Shakespeare as their primary literary reference point, and hence more likely than others to be cited as first user (Gray 1986), he is commonly credited with coining many English words and phrases still in use. For this reason alone, to study Shakespeare is to study the stuff with which millions of people's thoughts are made, and a Marxist approach would be to consider what kinds of things can scarcely be said, or may only be said with convoluted periphrasis, because of this: in other words, what kind of rhetoric is made possible, and what kind made difficult, using the language we inherited from our predecessors.

Class, Consciousness, and Ideology

A person's class is sometimes spoken of as though it were a personal attribute like sexual orientation, race, or gender, but the analogy is misleading for Marx's work uncovered how class came about and how it might be ended in the future. Like Marxism, gay studies, postcolonial theory, and feminism indulge in utopian thinking about the ending of oppression, but unlike it they do not seek to abolish the conditions that gave rise to the subject positions they promote. A Marxist approach to Shakespeare studies might confine itself to the study of impoverished characters such as the Apothecary in *Romeo and Juliet* or the ordinary soldiers in *Henry V* who 'sell the pasture now to buy the horse' (2.0.5) and need to capture French soldiers for the ransom they will pay. However, this would be a neglect of some of the most fruitful aspects of Marxist theory, for it was not merely fellow feeling for the oppressed that drove Marx but also a sense that he was uncovering fundamental historical principles.

A Marxist insight has taken hold throughout literary studies: that the origin of ideas, the 'definite forms of social consciousness' (or superstructure), can be found in the conditions that gave rise to them, the 'relations of production' that are 'the real foundation' (or base) (Marx 1970, 20–1). The base/superstructure model was Marx's first account of ideology, and it is here that Marxism lays claim to the entire world of artistic production. Unfortunately, at times Marx appears to have meant by ideology a set of untrue or distracting beliefs that prevent workers from seeing their exploitation (false consciousness, as Engels later put it), and at other times he uses it to mean the collective beliefs of the ruling class, which dominate society's intellectual life just as the ruling class's purposes hold sway in practice. These two senses are scarcely compatible with each other or the base/superstructure model, since if consciousness arises out of social being then it is true to that social being (so not a false consciousness), whereas if it is false it is difficult to see why the ruling class—whom no one is trying to dupe—would believe it. To add confusion, Marx appears to also use the word ideology in the sense of a scientific, or pseudo-scientific, study of superstructural processes, so that we may speak of a Marxist ideology just as easily as a Fascist one. The later works of Marx provided a not entirely satisfying explanation for these contradictory uses of the word by arguing that misrepresentation and distortion are structural effects of capitalism, so that the contradiction originates in the economic base and is projected onto the superstructure, which thus exhibits self-contradiction.

The word 'ideology' originally meant the investigation of where ideas come from, their specific scientific and historical determinants (Gramsci 1971, 375–7; Eagleton 1991, 63–70), but has come to have one distinct meaning in common usage, that of rigidly held political doctrines that prevent those who hold them from seeing the world clearly, and another in academic circles, that of a set of unspoken, even unconscious, assumptions about the world that help us make sense of it. In either sense, ideas are not free-floating entities with an independent life of their own (the ultra-Idealist view), but rather they are tied to how life is, or might be, lived.

The young Marx was much concerned with philosophy, especially idealism, and his break from this was lived as a break from his former friends in the Young Hegelians movement, Ludwig Feuerbach, Bruno Bauer, and Max Stirner. In the preface to *The German Ideology*, co-written with Engels, Marx stated his aim as the exposure of the middle-class preoccupations of the Young Hegelians, especially their valorization of ideas:

Once upon a time a valiant fellow had the idea that men were drowned in water only because they were possessed with the *idea of gravity*. . . . His whole life long he fought against the illusion of gravity, of whose harmful results all statistics brought him new and manifold evidence. This honest fellow was the type of the new revolutionary philosophers in Germany. (Marx and Engels 1974, 37)

The Young Hegelians put ideas before reality and Marx came to see his own philosophical work as likewise flawed in its concern with categories and abstractions rather than life as it is lived, and hence Marx's insistence in his base/superstructure model that reality shapes ideas, that social being shapes consciousness.

In Marx's materialist historicism it is not how people and their social relations appear to themselves or others (the superstructure) that shapes social forms and relations, but how they really are related in production (the base). The superstructure 'of ideas, of conceptions, of consciousness' cannot exceed the limits set by the base, because people's ideas are 'the direct efflux of their material behaviour', are the 'sublimates of their material life-process', so that 'Life is not determined by consciousness, but consciousness by life' (Marx and Engels 1974, 47). Marx distanced himself from the Empiricists, who make a collection of dead facts, and from the Idealists, who deal in the imagined activity of imagined subjects, and he put life as it is actually lived at the centre of his historical method. In this method, philosophy loses its status as a separate activity. To make history one must eat, feed, and stay warm, so the first historical act is 'the production of material life itself' (Marx and Engels 1974, 48). As soon as the basic needs are satisfied, new needs are created and satisfied and thus history begins. From family relations develop complex social relations based on more complex production to satisfy wants, and hence history must be founded on analysis of production, how it happens, and how people organize to achieve it.

It was not possible or desirable for Marx to jettison all of his philosophical study, but apparently he was convinced that a number of Gordian knots could be cut. Consciousness, for example, Marx simply conflated with language: both arose from our need for intercourse with other people, and both are thus inherently social. The first thing consciousness perceived was nature and it was terrifyingly alien and indomitable, so humankind invented religion. Here one can clearly see consciousness determined by social being: as nature came under humankind's control, we ceased to have animalistic blind awe towards it. Increased productivity brought division of labour (initiated in the division of labour in sex) and, crucially, the division of physical from mental labour. At this point consciousness could have an independent life because it became able to reflect on something other than the real world. Now it could make '"pure" theory, theology, philosophy, ethics, etc.' (Marx and Engels 1974, 52).

However, ideas are not, Marx insisted, the driving force of historical change; that role was played by the 'productive forces', meaning the capacity to make things. A capacity to produce things exists within a given set of prevailing conditions, the available materials, tools, and knowledge, but also (and crucially) the way people get together to do the making, or their 'forms of intercourse'. In a difficult and compressed paragraph Marx outlined his view of historical progress that would become known as 'historical materialism':

These various conditions, which appear first as conditions of self-activity, later as fetters upon it, form in the whole evolution of history a series of forms of intercourse, the coherence of which consists in this: in the place of an earlier form of intercourse, which has become a fetter, a new one is put, corresponding to the more developed productive forces and, hence, to the advanced mode of the self-activity of individuals—a form which in its turn becomes a fetter and then is replaced by another. Since these conditions correspond at every stage to the simultaneous development of the productive forces, their history is at the same time the history of the evolving productive forces taken over by each new generation, and is, therefore, the history of the development of the forces of the individuals themselves. (Marx and Engels 1974, 87)

Putting production at the centre of his historical model, Marx saw that people naturally form associations one with another to improve the quality and quantity of what they make, and necessarily form allegiances and groupings to do so. These groupings get larger and larger until they can rightly be called classes and recorded history is full of class struggles, each of which erupts in a revolution that changes forever their relationships and their compositions. After a revolution the new arrangements allow production to increase, but the ever-expanding productive forces again outgrow the forms of intercourse and what was once a liberation of productive forces becomes, in its turn, a fetter on production that must be broken in another revolution. From the quotation above one might think the process to be endless, but it is in fact finite and has, in the industrialized West, reached its penultimate stage in which there are just two classes, the huge and increasing proletariat (who own virtually nothing) and the small and diminishing bourgeoisie (who own virtually everything). The logical end of the process is for the former to expropriate the latter, and run things for the benefit of themselves (which means everyone): 'With the appropriation of the total productive forces through united individuals, private property comes to an end' (Marx and Engels 1974, 93).

The explanation that Marx offered in *The German Ideology* was that the ideology (ideas, institutions, and practices) of any society is whatever is necessary to maintain its way of life, so for example maritime law was developed first by the merchants of the medieval town of Amalfi because it was the first to carry on extensive trade (Marx and Engels 1974, 80). However, if ideas are simply in the service of production, it is difficult to see how societies could change, and *The German Ideology* is much concerned with the different ideologies that accompanied slave-owning societies, feudalism, and capitalism. Marx knew that he was in trouble with his model of ideas coming after doing: '[Marxist history] does not explain practice from the idea but explains the formation of ideas from material practice' and so 'the practical overthrow of the actual social relations' is what it takes to change ideas (Marx and Engels 1974, 58). Thus, '[Marxist history] shows that

circumstances make men just as much as men make circumstances'
(Marx and Engels 1974, 59).

The problem is to reconcile this with the obvious place that ideas
have *in* the circumstances, for Marx was well aware that there is no
such thing as mere 'doing' without preceding ideas that help us decide
what to do and how to do it. Ideas are built into practices, so that, for
example, overthrowing the banking system of Western capitalism
could not be achieved by massed armed robbery of all the paper money
in the vaults, because that money would be worthless paper without a
social convention based on trust, the confidence we display in
accepting paper money because we believe that later we will be able
to exchange it for something useful (Marx and Engels 1974, 90). This
would appear, then, to be a case of the superstructure, the ideas about
paper money, being part of the base, the economic reality, so the base/
superstructure distinction is here partly deconstructed. Moreover, in
order for there to be epochal change, Marx wanted to assert that ideas
could be historically in advance of economic reality so that the base
becomes a fetter that is holding back progress; beyond a certain point
this tension breaks and a whole new way of organizing production (say
feudalism instead of slavery, or capitalism instead of feudalism) comes
into being. Clearly, this model of economic reality catching up with
the superstructure sits awkwardly with the assertion that the superstructure is the set of ideas and practices necessary for (and produced
by) the economic base.

Worse, there are parts of *The German Ideology* where Marx appears
to treat ideology as not simply the necessary ideas thrown up by a way
of economic life, but as a weapon used by one class against another:
'The ideas of the ruling class are in every epoch the ruling ideas, i.e. the
class which is the ruling *material* force of society, is at the same time its
ruling *intellectual* force' (Marx and Engels 1974, 64). Yet Marx immediately followed this with an assertion that some people can avoid sub-
ordination to the ruling ideas—'The existence of revolutionary ideas
in a particular period presupposes the existence of a revolutionary
class . . .' (Marx and Engels 1974, 65)—and then switched back to the
notion of ideology as deception foisted on everyone by the ruling class,
which 'has to give its ideas the form of universality, and represent them
as the only rational, universally valid ones' (Marx and Engels 1974, 66).
It is impossible to reconcile these assertions, for the elegant simplicity

of the base/superstructure model resides in its accounting for the totality of ideas thinkable in a period by linking this to how production is organized; by admitting the principle of conflict between the ruling ideas and the revolutionary ones Marx lapsed back into the idealism he so earnestly tried to avoid. To see why, we only have to ask 'Where do the revolutionary ideas come from?' If from the economic base, they should be the same as the ruling ideas that they confront, and if from elsewhere then the economic base is not the sole source of ideas.

Marx later developed a more sophisticated model of ideology, presented in the first volume of *Capital*, and it addressed the above problems. The keys to this new model were reification, commodity fetishism, and alienation. A commodity is a particular kind of product that has no individual identifying features but rather is entirely like another of the same kind. A hand-made chair and a custom-built sports car are not commodities, precisely because they are supposed to be individualized, while barrels of oil and mass-produced cars are commodities inasmuch as they can be traded collectively by 'amount'. Nobody on the trading floor of a commodities market asks which particular barrels of oil they are buying since any are as good as the next. In developed societies, Marx observed, commodities are made for the purpose of being exchanged and this has an effect on those making them.

There is ordinarily an important psychical bond between a maker and the things she makes, so that creators feel that something of themselves has been invested in their creations. Making things solely for the purpose of exchanging them in an entirely impersonal way severs this bond in taking away the distinctiveness of the products, and the only question for producers becomes 'How much of something else will I get for my product?' Once the exchange ratios become settled, they start to feel oddly like inherent properties in the products themselves (gold just feels 100,000 times more valuable than corn), and when the ratios vary over time it feels like the products are alive. For the producers '... their own social action takes the form of the action of objects, which rule the producers instead of being ruled by them' (Marx 1954, 79); and although underneath all the fluctuations is the principle that value is the amount of labour that went into a thing, knowing this does not prevent the fluctuations looking like a chaotic storm created by the objects themselves (Marx 1954, 80).

Labour of all kinds originates in the human body and mind, and is in that sense equal, but all labour is also equal in that it creates in objects a value that can be quantified, and these objects enter into relationships that take the form of the social relations between the producers. Unlike other products, a commodity is mysterious 'because in it the social character of men's labour appears to them as an objective character stamped upon the product of that labour; because the relation of the producers to the sum total of their own labour is presented to them as a social relation, existing not between themselves, but between the products of their labour' (Marx 1954, 77). Ordinarily one's creations are closely tied to one's experiences and achievements, and human beings naturally form strong emotional ties to things they make; they may even fetishize them. The commodity system destroys this natural emotional tie and unnaturally fetishizes something else entirely: the abstract principle of exchange. Marx likened this inversion of the immanent and the contingent, the natural and the social, to the inversions of Dogberry in Shakespeare's *Much Ado About Nothing*, for whom 'To be a well-favoured man is the gift of fortune, but to write and read comes by nature' (3.3.13–15), as in bourgeois thinking commodities seem to have use-value (say, the pleasure I get from consuming an ice cream) and exchange-value (what I have to do to get an ice cream) built in to them, whereas in truth these things are human constructs (Marx 1954, 87).

The process of projecting the intangible, the social, the human into material objects is reification, and this is what happens with the production of commodities: relationships between people are mysteriously transformed into relationships between these inanimate objects. The producer of a commodity will experience this as a severing of her bond with what she makes so that it comes to seem like a hostile and impersonal force ranged against her; because of this she feels alienated not only from the fruit of her labour but from her labour itself. These thoughts on alienated labour are first recorded in incomplete manuscripts from 1844 on the connection between economics and philosophy (Marx 1977, 61–74), and they provided Marx with a new way to think about ideology: alienation happens in production, at the economic base, and spreads into the superstructure from there. Alienation is a form of mystification, making it hard to see the human activities of labour and production, and this serves to naturalize the present way of doing things because labour and production lose their social appearance and seem merely the consequences of the way objects in the world naturally relate to one another. Thus deception is built into capitalist production, it does not have to be a separate activity that serves it, and it begins not in consciousness but in material production. Rather than ideology being 'false consciousness' (a phrase coined by Engels in a letter to Franz Mehring in 1893), or a con-trick played on the gullible workers, it is a structural effect of capitalism.

This new view of ideology does not solve all the problems of the old one given in *The German Ideology*. For one thing, it seems to do away with the need for a superstructure at all, linking production directly to consciousness without requiring a realm of ideas and institutions to mediate it. For another, it seems to make ideology specific to one kind of economic system, capitalism with its exchange of commodities, which rather implies that there was no ideology in earlier societies and there will be none in the socialist future. Also it still does not properly account for historical change, for Marxism itself is a set of ideas that, by its own theory, is not distorted by capitalism but rather sees reality clearly; so not *all* thought is distorted by the fracturing processes of reification and alienation.

This is a serious problem for Marxism since any claim that ideas entirely follow from economic needs necessarily cuts the ground out from under itself as a set of ideas. This is a version of the well-known Liar Paradox invoked by a generalizing that includes itself in its purview: the declaration 'I always lie' includes itself, so if it is true it must be false. The same paradox occurs with such popular postmodern generalizations as 'There are no universal truths', which if true excludes itself as a possible universal truth, and hence the assertion is false and thus there must indeed be some universal truths.

One might try to solve this problem by saying that Marxism is a scientific truth free from the distortions that afflict other kinds of thinking, but to admit this is to say that not all thought is determined by economic reality, so the initial insight of the base/superstructure relation has been lost. After all, if Marxism can be exempted from determination then perhaps other parts of the superstructure can be too, and thence anyone might argue that their beliefs escape determination. Alternatively, one might say that Marxism is a distinct kind of thinking generated by capitalism at a certain stage in its history, so that it is a determined thought but one selected by history to intervene at the point when it is needed. This keeps the principle of determination, but at the cost of losing Marxism's truth-claim that gives us a reason to prefer it to all other kinds of determined thought.

Twentieth-century Marxists grappled with the problem that an attempt to explain social reality by economics must stand somewhat apart from reality, and yet it needs to figure itself into the reality that it seeks to change. What follows here is a condensation of Terry Eagleton's brilliant analysis of how these dilemmas were addressed by Georg Lukács, Antonio Gramsci, Theodor Adorno, Herbert Marcuse, and Louis Althusser (Eagleton 1991, 33–159). If Marxism is part of social reality, how can it possibly model that same social reality without invoking an infinite regression like someone holding a mirror up to another mirror and seeing an uncountable number of reflections? Georg Lukács proposed a solution based on reification itself, since although this dehumanizes the worker and 'cripples and atrophies his "soul"', yet 'his humanity and his soul are not changed into commodities'; on the contrary, the fusing of the worker with her oppression is '*subjectively* the point at which this structure [i.e. base] is raised to consciousness and where it can be breached in practice' (Lukács 1971, 172). In this quotation, Lukács, like other Marxists, favoured the term structure/superstructure instead of base/superstructure in order to avoid suggesting that economic production is simpler, more 'basic', than the superstructure it generates. The consciousness of the proletariat, when it fully comes about, will be effectively the self-consciousness of the process that dehumanizes them, so that unlike other groups that are misled by reification, '... the proletariat [will] become the identical subject-object of history whose praxis will change reality' (Lukács 1971, 197).

The proletariat has a universal quality about it for another reason too: it grows so huge in late capitalism that there is virtually no one else but the workers and a tiny class of bourgeoisie, and by overthrowing the bourgeoisie the proletariat repeats what all previous revolutions have done—putting a new class in power—while simultaneously ending that process because the new ruling class *is* everyone. Equally, just prior to this overthrow, the consciousness of the proletariat is the consciousness of virtually everyone, so in that sense too it is a universal subjectivity, which is the same thing as objectivity. Neat as this solution is, the Liar Paradox has not been entirely circumvented, for if, as Lukács claimed, the proletariat alone bears true class consciousness (its subjectivity being universal, and hence objective), from where is that assertion made? Not from within class consciousness (since there must be an existing notion of 'truth' if the proletarian class consciousness is to embody it) and yet not from outside either, because outside it there is only untruth.

Antonio Gramsci addressed the problem by expanding the question to consider how the ruling class elicits consent to its rule, which phenomenon includes ideology but also many other means, and for this expanded notion he employed the term hegemony. Gramsci was concerned with civil society, the institutions that mediate between the state and the economy, and decided that it is these that elicit consent while the state itself has the monopoly on coercive violence via the army, the police, and the penal system. Any ruling class, of course, has to elicit consent rather than just use coercion, but capitalism especially relies on consent since use of force would put its rule up for contestation; the marketplace principle of freely associating individuals exchanging labour and money must seem to be governing all social relations. Ideology functions at the psychological level so that each individual internalizes the social order's governing principles and lives them as though they were her own (which, being so deeply embedded, they are).

In *Prison Notebooks* (written 1929–35 and published posthumously), Gramsci argued that the word ideology has been debased by misuse and that we must 'distinguish between historically organic ideologies, those, that is, which are necessary to a given structure [i.e. base], and ideologies that are arbitrary, rationalistic, or "willed"' (Gramsci 1971, 376–7). For Gramsci, no form of consciousness is good for all time, and Marxism is just the form of consciousness necessary to the present state of affairs. Subordinated groups live a contradiction between official, ruling-class, ideology and their own experience, but the latter tends to be incomplete and confused until the class acts as an 'organic totality' and makes its own coherent world view—somewhat like Lukács's sense of the universal subjectivity of the proletariat—and this can come about by the action of intellectuals like himself who, no matter what their actual professions, are organic in 'directing the ideas and aspirations of the class to which they organically belong' (Gramsci 1971, 3).

The organic intellectual, unlike the traditional one, knows that ideas come from social life, and indeed the traditional intellectual's assertion that his ideas are independent was itself an idea that suited the ruling class, or put another way the claim to be free of ideology is itself ideological because it suits the ruling class. In relation to Shakespeare, two critics have recently argued that the disconnectedness of art, Oscar Wilde's principle of *ars gratia artis*, is one we can see coming into being in the Renaissance. Richard Wilson found that Shakespeare's drama, unlike that of his contemporaries, strives to deny its own commercial origins by imagining unfettered aristocratic patronage, even to the point of casting the Globe's yardling audience as 'gentles' in *Henry V* (Pro. 8, 2.0.35), but in *The Tempest* Shakespeare finally admits that aristocratic patronage is necessarily constraining (Wilson 2001). In the same volume of essays, Scott Cutler Shershow considered the mental back-flips that were necessary to make sense of the biblical Parable of the Talents, which seems to be a justification of usury in its praise for the servant who multiplies his five talents and condemnation of the servant who buries his own (Matthew 25: 14–29). In particular Shershow considered how 'talent' in our modern sense of inherent quality (as opposed to a unit of money) was invented to serve this need and brought a splitting of the temporal and spiritual domains, each having its own rules. Eventually the principle of investment-and-return was accepted in both domains, but to compensate for the capitulation the author had to be figured as the ultimate gift-giver, and hence the modern view that Shakespeare is infinitely abundant and Marxist criticism is narrow and partial (Shershow 2001).

A common principle in Marxist explanations of consciousness, culture, and art is that what goes on in the economic base makes its way into the superstructure, and we have seen how for Lukács and Gramsci this meant that the psychical split created by alienation runs all the way through bourgeois society. At the Institute for Social Research in Frankfurt, Germany, founded in 1923, a group of thinkers attempted to apply Marxism to an interdisciplinary study of social theory, and a common finding among them was that in fact the principle of equivalence in commodity exchange is what spreads throughout capitalist society, so that in theory at least bourgeois culture holds each person to be the same for the purposes of law, voting rights, and property. This equivalence masks a deeper difference between people, for the law is actually constructed to favour the propertied over the poor, but the so-called Frankfurt School (which effectively decamped to Columbia University during the Second World War) had considerable success with the idea of 'false equivalence'. It is false not only because it is deceptive (people are actually heterogeneous, just as is the labour that goes into making commodities), but also because it reduces everything to the bland sameness of consumerist uniformity dressed up as choice. (The late-twentieth century anti-capitalist movement was much motivated by rejection of consumerist uniformity, and its most visible expression, McDonald's fast-food outlets, are prime targets for rioters. It would be as well to note that the principle of uniformity is double-edged, and that for all his power and wealth Bill Gates cannot buy a Big Mac better than yours or mine.)

Theodor Adorno of the Frankfurt School argued in *Negative Dialectics* (in German, 1966) that the ideological impulse to homogenize is the effect of a hatred of the different that arose in our ancestors from biological need: to kill prey a predator needs rage and as we became human this was rationalized and sublimated, creating the unconscious 'ideology that the not-I, *l'autrui* . . . is inferior' (Adorno 1973, 23). Bourgeois society has a central antinomy, since 'To preserve itself, to remain the same, to "be", that society must constantly expand, progress, advance its frontiers, not respect any limit, not remain the same' (Adorno 1973, 26), and is built upon a principle that constantly seeks to reduce heterogeneity: ' . . . it is through barter that non-identical individuals and performances become commensurable and identical. The spread of the principle imposes on the whole world an obligation to become identical, to become total' (Adorno 1973, 146). What cannot be claimed for identity is expelled as other, and one of the few places this simple dichotomizing is resisted is 'Radical modern art' (Adorno 1973, 95). The title of Herbert Marcuse's *One-Dimensional Man* (1964), a key text for anti-establishment struggles in the 1960s, indicated his agreement that capitalist ideology suppresses all contradiction in its valorization of uniformity and conformity. Terry Eagleton pointed out that this Frankfurt School Marxist view of ideology's homogeneity is wrong—in truth capitalism is quite content with liberal plurality and yet it must always contend with the social conflict it generates—but it must have seemed right to thinkers fleeing from Nazism (Eagleton 1991, 127–8).

The most influential Marxist writer on ideology has been Louis Althusser, who combined Lacanian psychoanalysis with bits of Gramsci's work in his celebrated essay 'Ideology and Ideological State Apparatuses' (Althusser 1971, 127–86). What Althusser called a 'problematic' (like a Foucauldian 'episteme') is a mental organization of categories at any given historical moment that limit what we can say and think. The closed, self-confirming nature of the problematic means that its ideological part is always returning us to the same answers to new questions—it forestalls new surprising answers—whereas pure science always threatens to break out of this enclosure and is genuinely exploratory.

Thus, unusually for a Western Marxist, Althusser treated science (including Marxist theory) as a discipline or epistemology unto itself, its discoveries being true no matter who holds them nor when, and this view contrasts with the historicist Marxists who think that theory is validated or invalidated by historical practice. For Althusser, ideology was not so much a deception that masks truth from us, but more a matter of feelings and experiences, a set of lived relations with the world that make us feel as though we are needed. These lived relations give each of us the impression that the world is addressing us individually, 'hailing' us as Althusser put it. In his model of the Mirror Stage, Jacques Lacan described how an infant sees its reflection, misrecognizes itself as more unified than it is, and merges with this image in a marriage of subject and object (Lacan 1977, 1–7). Likewise in Althusser's model we misrecognize ourselves in the image that ideology presents to us, and we answer its call to us, and feel bonded within a system that is in fact indifferent to us; in truth any number of other people could fill our roles in society. This is not exactly a deception, for the falsehood is necessary to functioning in society, and indeed Althusser made the even grander claim that each of us is called into being as a subject by being hailed by ideology, a process he called interpellation.

There are several problems with this claim, not least of which is that it just does not feel as though ideology called my thinking self into being; rather, the other way around seems right: we subjects created ideology with our minds. Also, if I came into being as a subject by responding to having been 'hailed' by ideology, what was I before and how in this earlier state did I have enough subjectivity to recognize and answer the call? One solution to these problems is to follow the lead of Saussure and Lacan in calling upon an analogy with language. For Althusser, ideology existed before I was born and with my emergence into the world it ran its energies through me to make me what I am, just as for Saussure and Lacan the pre-existing structure of the *langue* was the element into which I was born and which, before I had a chance to object, shaped my thoughts. After all, I made no conscious decision to think in English, this was simply determined by the prevailing custom where I was born, and as we saw above regarding the French ability to shock by misusing the word 'beef', this gives shape to the thoughts I can have and the arguments I can raise. By an analogous kind of deeply embedded activity, Althusser argued, the ideological state apparatuses (church, school, the media, the arts) shaped my mind so that the repressive state apparatuses (the armed forces, the police, the law courts) seldom have to compel me to support capitalism.

Chapters 2 and 3 of this book will explore in detail how Marxist thinking about production, ideology, and culture shaped twentieth-century Shakespeare studies, but for the purpose of introduction the above general principles will serve, and we can return to Shakespeare's time and his art to see how the principles might illuminate the plays.

Renaissance Ideology and Language in Shakespeare's *Richard II*

The historical Richard II's right to rule England was based on his familial relation to his grandfather Edward III, but he was succeeded by Henry Bolingbroke who took the throne by force to become Henry IV. Thus was broken a principle of succession by inheritance, and one of the attractions of Shakespeare's play *Richard II* is its dramatization of how this came about. In his famous speech about the natural state of England ('this sceptred isle . . . This other Eden, demi-paradise') John of Gaunt makes specific allegations that under Richard the country itself

> Is now leased out—I die pronouncing it—
> Like to a tenement or pelting farm.
> England . . .
> . . . is now bound in with shame,
> With inky blots and rotten parchment bonds.

> (2.1.59–64)

Editors of the play are unanimous that here Richard is accused of forming an economic arrangement with his subjects regarding the land, and that this abnegates his responsibility towards it, for a tenement farm is one rented, not owned, by the farmer who works it. This changes the king's status from supreme ruler above the law to mere subject of it:

> [JOHN OF GAUNT]
> Landlord of England art thou now, not king.
> Thy state of law is bondslave to the law,
>
> (2.1.113–14)

Gaunt characterizes such contractual arrangements as rotten and a stain on England's character. Richard hastens to the dying Gaunt to seize the valuables that would otherwise pass to his son Bolingbroke, so Gaunt's attack forms part of a larger pattern of Richard's disruption of ancient practices for the transference of wealth. Willoughby follows the same economic theme in citing as a reason for rebellion against Richard his use of 'blanks' (documents promising the king unspecified amounts of money), and the play is insistently concerned with the paper form of these arrangements.

In Gaunt's reference to 'rotten parchment bonds', the stress is presumably on 'parchment', the reification of an obligation, for aristocratic culture is familiar with immaterial bonds. Indeed, the play begins with one:

> KING RICHARD
> Old John of Gaunt, time-honoured Lancaster,
> Hast thou according to thy oath and bond
> Brought hither Henry Hereford, thy bold son,
>
> (1.1.1–3)

Here Gaunt's oath is his bond, it needs no literalization in a contract, and even under extreme pressure men of this class reach not for a document but a symbol to make concrete their words. When Fitzwalter accuses Aumerle of treason he throws down his glove, gauntlet, or hood and says 'There is my bond of faith / To tie thee to my strong correction' (4.1.67–8). So many men accuse Aumerle that the scene descends into comedy generated by the way a gage (a sign) combines immaterial meaning with material presence, so that having exhausted his supply in an orgy of gage-throwing Aumerle is forced to borrow one to continue his denials (4.1.74).

Aumerle is tainted by his close association with deposed king Richard and his well-known dislike of Bolingbroke, and continuing the contrast between immaterial, eternal bonds and those realized in paper, Aumerle's involvement in the conspiracy to restore Richard is discovered by his father's noticing the seal hanging from a document Aumerle is carrying. In the document the conspirators have 'interchangeably set down their hands' (5.2.98) to kill King Henry. Aumerle's mother does not understand how bonds work:

> DUCHESS OF YORK   What should you fear?
>   'Tis nothing but some bond that he is entered into
>   For gay apparel 'gainst the triumph day.
> YORK
>   Bound to himself? What doth he with a bond
>   That he is bound to? Wife, thou art a fool.

> (5.2.64–8)

Standing in for an obligation, a bond (like a modern IOU) was held by the person to whom the obligation was owed (Sokol and Sokol 2000, 'bond'), and as a material object the capitalist bond could be dissolved by tearing the paper that embodies it—'Take thrice thy money. Bid me tear the bond' (*The Merchant of Venice*, 4.1.231)—while the older immaterial bond is more durable precisely because it is not embodied. (An analogous relation underlies the play's several meditations on the nature of a king's 'sentence' in 1.3, for speech is, paradoxically, more permanent than writing: once uttered, spoken words cannot be destroyed.) Like the bond in *The Merchant of Venice*, the bonds in *Richard II* seem to suggest a reification of obligations that corresponds to the replacement of a feudal set of values with their proto-capitalist substitutes, by which reading Richard's deposition is initiated by his own error of hastening the capitalist age in replacing immaterial ancient rights with material contracts.

There is a problem with this reading of *Richard II*, since from a Marxist view—predicated on the forward progression of historical epochs categorized by their organization of production (slavery, feudalism, capitalism, socialism)—we would expect to find Bolingbroke, Richard's successor, embodying the new capitalistic principle. The straightforward Marxist view is offered by David Margolies in a study of the play's representations of the disintegration of social structures:

> King Richard and Bolingbroke are more than two individuals in conflict; they are made to represent a struggle between hierarchical and individualistic world-views.... The principle of the individual vanquishes the principle of hierarchy; the right of ownership defeats the right of authority.
>
> The two sets of principles are incompatible: there is no way in which Bolingbroke's victory and his principle of ownership could be justified in the terms of the old inherited principles of the country. (Margolies 1992, 144–5)

Here 'world-views' means roughly ideologies, and Bolingbroke represents progress.

If, as Margolies maintained, Bolingbroke represents progress, what are we to make of the 'inky blots' by which the old order is stained with the textual practices of the new? Frequently Shakespeare has characters refer to personal imperfections as 'spots', and they are 'black and grainèd' for a self-reflecting Gertrude (*Hamlet*, 3.4.80) and indelible for a psychotic Lady Macbeth (*Macbeth*, 5.1.33). Just occasionally, however, spottedness can be a guarantee of identity, as with Innogen's 'cinque-spotted' mole that none but Posthumus should know (*Cymbeline*, 2.2.38) and Mowbray's insubordinate resistance to Richard's 'Lions make leopards tame' with 'Yea, but not change his spots' (*Richard II*, 1.1.174–5). The idea of a leopard's skin being the site of its unchangeable nature is in tension with our modern sense that identity is a matter of the internal and unseen, but Mowbray insists that identity is necessarily outside the body in the form of 'spotless reputation', without which 'Men are but gilded loam, or painted clay' (1.1.178–9). The choice here is between two forms of perfected outside, an immaterial representation in the minds of others (reputation) and a merely material covering of showy gold. Much of the play hinges on Richard's spottedness, his failure to live up to the ideal of kingship (a perfected humanity), and characters repeatedly liken the ideal monarch to the golden sun.

This metaphor need not draw on alchemical thinking since ordinary ideas about value and purity are sufficient to explain it; however, the alchemists' understanding of the transformative power of the sun lent the sun/king association additional weight because the sun's rays, penetrating the earth, were thought to provide 'the generative warmth to ripen such imperfect metals as iron, copper and lead into the perfect metal, gold' (Abraham 1998, 'sun'). When Richard's Welsh followers give up on his return from Ireland, Salisbury imagines that Richard's 'sun sets weeping in the lowly west' (2.4.21); Bolingbroke in mid-rebellion sees Richard as a 'blushing discontented sun' (3.3.62) about to be obscured by clouds; defeated Richard wishes Bolingbroke 'many years of sunshine days' (4.1.211) before imagining himself a king of snow melting before 'the sun of Bolingbroke' (4.1.251); and in his own reflection Richard sees the face 'That like the sun did make beholders wink' (4.1.274).

The sun/king rhetoric of the play has been much noted, but before it has even got off the ground it is undercut in the first act by Boling-broke, who responds to banishment by observing that the sun will still shine on him and the 'golden beams to you here lent / Shall point on me and gild my banishment' (1.3.140–1). Thus Bolingbroke invokes the sun/king association before anyone else has a chance to use it, and by linking it with Mowbray's dismissal of mere gold-plating, Boling-broke slyly suggests that a king has only the exterior signs and golden trappings of power, which are available to anyone. For audience members who knew the ensuing history this was proleptic because Bolingbroke goes on to replace Richard and find the same danger alighting on himself: when kingship is treated as a possession not a right, the institution is fatally weakened. The point of a king being like the sun and like gold is that these things were held to be unchangeable, having reached a state of perfection seldom attained in the sublunary sphere. As the rebellion gathers head an alternative, unflattering, sun/king rhetoric emerges: Northumberland invokes the gold-plated trappings of kingship as he exhorts his peers to redeem the 'blemished crown' and 'Wipe off the dust that hides our sceptre's gilt' (2.1.295–6). In spoken performance there is no way of distinguishing between this kind of gilt and the guilt of Richard's wrongdoing, and indeed the first five editions of the play spelt the word 'guilt'.

In this reading, taciturn Bolingbroke gains the upper hand not because he is a silent man of action against a wordy effeminate poet, but because he understands the rhetoric of monarchical power and is able to reinvent it for his own purposes. This personal project, how-ever, is also a social project because it involves a new conception of the authority of kingship. Richard's view, and arguably the standard medieval view, is that the king is 'the deputy elected by the Lord' (3.2.53), meaning God, so this is authority descending from above. However, Bolingbroke is able to take the throne because of the popular support deriving from his reported 'courtship to the common people' in which 'Off goes his bonnet to an oysterwench' and 'A brace of draymen bid God speed him well' (1.4.23, 30–1); while of Richard it is said by his enemies that 'The commons hath he pilled with grievous taxes, / And quite lost their hearts' (2.1.247–8) and even his flatterers agree (2.2. 127–32). One might almost say that Bolingbroke's victory is a demo-cratic achievement.

Kingship is like language in its dependence on common consent and shared principles that are barely conscious: the utterance 'My liege' is not so much a willed expression as a verbal tic, and the inferiority and deference that underlie it are likewise more a matter of habit than reasoning. Just as a linguistic sign embodies immaterial meaning in a material form, so the principle of divine right of kings gave the monarch a double nature: a material body that would die and an immortal part that would instantaneously fly to the next in line, and hence the performative contradiction of 'The king is dead, long live the king' (Kantorowicz 1957, 409–18). The parallel can be extended to the material embodiment of a play in the written form encountered by readers and the immaterial 'text' that is a performance of it, although here emerges an important difference regarding nomenclature that seems to have interested Shakespeare.

Scripts and their performances are grounded in language, but a script's speech prefixes are not to be spoken. For a theatre audience there is no one called Claudius in *Hamlet* (the name is never men-tioned) only 'the king', and the same is true of Duke Vincentio in *Measure for Measure*. An audience is untroubled by the tricky editorial problem of fixing the precise moment when Bolingbroke's speech prefix changes to King Henry and of deciding whether Richard's speech prefix changes in the same instant, but the problem itself goes to the heart of the play's concern with nomenclature and the analogy between dramatic art and politics. York describes Richard's following Bolingbroke in a public procession into London with a theatrical simile: 'As in a theatre ... After a well-graced actor leaves the stage' the spectators' eyes 'Are idly bent on him that enters next' (5.2.23–5). Anti-theatricalists complained that drama undermined

social hierarchy by implying that social identity (specifically, superiority) was merely a matter of costuming. A recurring theme of
Shakespeare's history plays is the related suggestion that politics is a
form of role-playing, and for the actor-king Bolingbroke the naming of
characters matters very much. The man who answered the question
'Who are you?' in the trial-by-combat of 1.3 with the list of places
('Harry of Hereford, Lancaster, and Derby', 1.3.35–6) changes his name
one last time in becoming King Henry, a renaming that robs Richard of
the title. York is caught in the middle of this epochal change:

> T'one is my sovereign, whom both my oath
> And duty bids defend; t'other again
> Is my kinsman, whom the King hath wronged,
>
> (2.2.112–14)

If we are looking for the play's binarial choices such as backward/
forward, medieval/Renaissance, feudalism/capitalism (and in purely
characterological terms wordy/taciturn, poetic/prosaic, passive/active,
and effeminate/masculinist), then York might stand for an indeter-
minate and wavering third term that is neither one thing nor another.
A pivotal moment of the plot is York's last, and merely verbal, stand
against Bolingbroke's rebellion, which is immediately followed by
capitulation:

> YORK
> Well, well, I see the issue of these arms.
> I cannot mend it, I must needs confess,
> Because my power is weak and all ill-left.
> But if I could, by Him that gave me life,
> I would attach you all, and make you stoop
> Unto the sovereign mercy of the King.
> But since I cannot, be it known to you
> I do remain as neuter. So fare you well—
> Unless you please to enter in the castle
> And there repose you for this night.
>
> (2.3.151–60)

The connotations of York's word 'neuter' are military (he lacks the
force to compel) and sexual (he feels emasculated), but also linguistic:
it is the gender of nouns that are neither masculine nor feminine; this

position seems intolerable and he collapses into passive support for the party of the future. In his social being, then, York has made the transition to the new order, but his superstructural linguistic practice seems to lag behind, and even after the audience has seen Richard's abdication York refers to 'the Duke, great Bolingbroke' (5.2.7). However, this is part of his description of the recent past—Bolingbroke's triumphant entrance into London with Richard following—so arguably York (like Shakespeare) is preserving the past nomenclature appropriate to the past events he describes. On the other hand, he concludes the story in the present tense ('To Bolingbroke are we sworn subjects now', 5.2.39), which rather suggests he simply cannot give up the old terminology. At a conscious level, though, York knows that with the new king comes a new naming practice, and he is more concerned to preserve it ('Aumerle that was...you must call him "Rutland" now', 5.2.41–3) than to preserve his own son, whose transgression he readily betrays to his new master. In Marxist terms, the superstructure is here revealed as inconsistent in a way that we could map onto a Freudian distinction between the unconscious and the conscious, and the character of York provides a study of the personal conflicts created when a man tries to suture the ideological rift created by epochal change.

Rather than treat York's conflict and betrayal of his son as tragedy, as well he might, Shakespeare opts for comedy: York races to denounce his son to King Henry, is overtaken by the offender, and is closely followed by his wife. (For a modern audience the striking analogues are denunciations under Nazism, Stalinism, and Maoism, making the comic tone difficult to sustain.) As we have seen, the play is much concerned with the relationship between linguistic and political power, with the 'breath of kings' (1.3.208) as a power to 'sentence' with a 'sentence'. Even critics hostile to Marxist readings tend to agree that Gaunt's famous speech imagining England to be a blessed island (a 'precious stone set in the silver sea', 2.1.46) can reasonably be called ideological because of its idealization and its denial of geographical reality: England is (and then was) actually only one part of an island (Great Britain) that also contains the countries of Scotland and Wales.

The proper context for this, however, is not so much England of the late fourteenth century as England of the late sixteenth century, a country still coming to terms with the loss of its last possession in

France when Calais fell to François de Lorraine, second duc de Guise in 1558. Shakespeare's history plays dwell on England's loss of French holdings, and Calais is the location for the originating treasons in *Richard II*: Mowbray is accused of misappropriating the Calais garrison's pay (1.1.87–132), and Mowbray and Aumerle are implicated in the murder of the Duke of Gloucester at Calais (1.1.100–3, 4.1.9–12, 4.1.71–3). With the contraction to a geographic unity (albeit one rather more internally heterogeneous than Gaunt's rhetoric acknowledges), and following the near catastrophe of the Spanish Armada, a proto-nationalism combining linguistic and ethnic realities emerges in the Shakespeare history plays' collective sense of England. French is not merely a different language but a context in which (as with 'boeuf' and 'beef') the differing distribution of signifiers can fundamentally alter the signified understood by the hearer of an utterance, as the Duchess of York finds as she pleads for her son's life:

> Say 'Pardon', King. Let pity teach thee how.
> The word is short, but not so short as sweet;
> No word like 'Pardon' for kings' mouths so meet.
> YORK
> Speak it in French, King: say 'Pardonnez-moi'.
> DUCHESS OF YORK
> Dost thou teach pardon pardon to destroy?
> Ah, my sour husband, my hard-hearted lord
> That sets the word itself against the word!
> Speak 'Pardon' as 'tis current in our land;
> The chopping French we do not understand.
>
> (5.3.114–22)

This is a struggle for meaning—a desperate desire to shape the king's 'sentence'—in which York counters the Duchess's plea for pardon with a French context (the phrase meaning 'Pardon me', that is, 'no I cannot') that reverses the sense. The Duchess insists on the proper context, the English one, but in saying that she does not understand French she reveals that she does, else she would not know what her husband had just proposed. The Marxist concern to emphasize contradiction (especially self-contradiction) resonates powerfully with latent concerns in Shakespeare's plays, and as we shall see much recent criticism has preferred to emphasize the dramatic power of such moments of discontinuity and rupture instead of attending to the artistic smoothness and closure identified by earlier criticism.

The reading of *Richard II* offered in this chapter is not exclusively a Marxist one, and similar things are said in works that take an eclectic approach under the rubrics of historicism, poststructuralism, and deconstruction. However, at origin these approaches (and more recent schools of thought) depend on Marxist thinking whose centrality to twentieth-century Shakespeare studies is under-appreciated. This book aims to show that, at their most powerful, recent forms of Shakespeare criticism are inherently Marxist—one might say that they are among the various forms that critical Marxism has taken on—and their vigour derives from a foundational rejection of the 'givens' of bourgeois culture. Those 'givens' are part of an absurd teleology that understands all previous historical change as progression towards the virtually unfettered free market in goods and services that we see across most of the world at the start of the twenty-first century. A survey of the influence of Marx's ideas on Shakespeare criticism is, at the same time, a history of reasoned rejections of such fatuity.

2

Marx's Influence on
Shakespeare Studies to 1968

> I never met Karl Marx personally but the people who have never
> read him now think him obsolete in order to justify their lack of
> knowledge. If it weren't for Karl Marx I might still have been
> writing unreadable novels.
>
> (G. B. Shaw, *Days with Bernard Shaw*, 1951)

A central theme of my argument is that Marx's ideas have pervaded all
aspects of Shakespeare criticism, theory, and performance, in ways not
fully appreciated. This chapter and the next one survey this process in
the afterlife of Marx's ideas, first via two influential Marxist theatre
practitioners and then in the wider realm of Shakespeare criticism. We
have surveyed enough of Marx's central body of ideas for the story of
their impact to be told roughly chronologically, with one exception:
Marxist dialectics. This aspect of his thinking was largely implicit in
Marx's writing, addressed directly only in *The Poverty of Philosophy* (in
French, 1847), and receiving little attention before Stalin's use of it in
the 1930s. Because dialecticism becomes important with the rise of
Stalin, an explanation of it is deferred until our story reaches the 1930s,
in the middle of this chapter.

G. B. Shaw's Marxism and Shakespeare

While Marx was working in the Reading Room of the British
Museum Library in the 1880s, George Bernard Shaw was there too
writing his early (unsuccessful) novels and anonymous reviews of

music, literature, and art. Shaw read Marx's *Capital* in 1883 and declared himself a convert, and joined the newly formed Fabian Society, named after the Roman general Fabius Cunctator, whose main strategy was to delay battle until the best possible moment for victory presented itself. The Fabians planned to permeate mainstream political and social institutions and press for change from within, and a frequent theme of Shaw's own writing on communism (later usefully compiled in his *The Intelligent Woman's Guide to Socialism and Capitalism*, 1928) was that elements of the proposed system—such as collective ownerships of roads and street-lamps—are already with us and cause no great alarm. Thus Shaw quickly had moved from a revolutionary to an evolutionary conception of socialism, in which the passing of particular laws within the present political structures of parliamentary democracy would secure a peaceful transition to communist utopia.

In the 'Note to . . .' his play *Caesar and Cleopatra* (first performed 1899) Shaw asserted his rejection of the idea of 'Progress with a capital P' because

> . . . in truth, the period of time covered by history is far too shallow to allow of any perceptible progress in the popular sense of Evolution of the Human Species. The notion that there has been any such Progress since Caesar's time (less than 20 centuries) is too absurd for discussion. All the savagery, barbarism, dark ages and the rest of it of which we have any record as existing in the past, exists at the present moment. (Shaw 1971, 295)

Despite his knowledge of Darwinian evolution, Shaw understood (in order to reject) the idea of progress only in the sense used by Macaulayan Whig history: the teleological view that all the strivings of people in the past were directed towards the goal of the present, or perhaps (a little less self-aggrandizingly) that everything past and present represents a collective striving towards a future goal of perfecting what we currently have. In fact, Darwinian evolutionary theory could account for incremental improvement without any sense of striving towards an endpoint, so that prehistoric cheetahs got faster at chasing gazelles and gazelles got better at spotting them afar off, without either species exerting effort towards a goal or being directed by a higher power. This point will be explored further in my conclusion.

Shaw believed that Shakespeare's philosophical impoverishment becomes apparent when one paraphrases his lines, a view announced while reviewing a production of *Much Ado About Nothing* (*'Shakespeare's Merry Gentlemen'* 26 *February* 1898*):*

When a flower-girl tells a coster to hold his jaw, for nobody is listening to him, and he retorts, 'Oh, youre there, are you, you beauty?' they reproduce the wit of Beatrice and Benedick exactly. But put it this way. 'I wonder that you will still be talking, Signior Benedick: nobody marks you.' 'What! my dear Lady Disdain, are you yet living?' You are miles from costerland at once. (Shaw 1932b, 323)

This claim that Shakespeare's distinctive power is in the particular 'music of the words' used to dress unimpressive ideas, his 'platitudes of proverbial philosophy', is typical Shaw. Shaw rightly perceived that communism begins from a conception of historical progress that he could not share, and in the preface to his play *Geneva* (first performed 1938) Shaw speculated that 'Had Marx and Engels been contemporaries of Shakespear they could not have written the Communist Manifesto, and would probably have taken a hand, as Shakespear did, in the enclosure of the common lands as a step forward in civilization' (Shaw 1974, 18–19). Putting Marx, Engels, and Shakespeare together like this is a mark of Shaw's sense that important individuals are somewhat in advance of their times. In a theatre review of 27 June 1896 ('The Second Dating of Sheridan') Shaw wrote that while ' . . . the difference between the institutions of the eighteenth and twentieth centuries may be as complete as the difference between a horse and a bicycle, the difference between men of those periods is only a trifling increment of efficiency, not nearly so great as that which differentiated Shakespear from the average Elizabethan' (Shaw 1932a, 166).

Thus two key observations by Shaw are in contradiction, for in imagining Marx and Engels as Shakespeare's contemporaries, Shaw denies them the power to think outside of the conceptual frameworks provided by the age—hence no *Communist Manifesto*—yet, Shaw insists that such great men are far ahead of the ideas of their age. Taking an average of Shaw's pronouncements on this head, he favours the former proposition over the latter, as when he reviewed a production of *Julius Caesar* ('Tappertit on Caesar', 29 January 1898): 'It is when we turn to Julius Caesar, the most splendidly written political melodrama we possess, that we realize the apparently immortal author of Hamlet as a man, not for all time, but for an age only, and that, too, in all solidly wise and heroic aspects, the most despicable of all the ages in our history' (Shaw 1932b, 298).

In the preface to his play *The Dark Lady of the Sonnets* (first performed 1910) Shaw gave the fullest account of his view of Shakespeare and it reveals how shallow his Marxism was. For Shaw the writing revealed the writer and, responding to a book about Shakespeare by his former editor at the *Saturday Review*, Frank Harris, Shaw satisfied himself about Shakespeare's social class (above the middle), Shakespeare's personality (excessive pessimism leavened with incorrigible gaiety), and Shakespeare's politics (a privateer) (Shaw 1972, 279–303). Where Harris saw a sycophant, Shaw drew on 'Not marble, nor the gilded monuments / Of princes, shall outlive this powerful rhyme' (Sonnet 55) to argue that 'A sycophant does not tell his patron that his fame will survive, not in the renown of his own actions, but in the sonnets of his sycophant' (Shaw 1972, 289, 295). Shaw's conception of a brave and cantankerous Shakespeare was drawn largely from the sonnets, but there was a particular accusation, that in his plays Shakespeare revealed himself 'an enemy of democracy', that Shaw was keen to dispel. The unflattering representations of ordinary people that we find in the plays are not political sentiments but plain speaking:

Everybody, including the workers themselves, know that they are dirty, drunken, foul-mouthed, ignorant, gluttonous, prejudiced: in short, heirs to the peculiar ills of poverty and slavery, as well as co-heirs with the plutocracy to all the failings of human nature. Even Shelley admitted, 200 years after Shakespeare wrote Coriolanus, that universal suffrage was out of the question. (Shaw 1972, 297)

Shaw rejected Harris's version of Shakespeare's life because it attached too little importance to the man's irony and gaiety: ' . . . all the bite, the impetus, the strength, the grim delight in his own power of looking terrible facts in the face with a chuckle, is gone; and you have nothing left but that most depressing of all things: a victim' (Shaw 1972, 290).

Yet to rescue Shakespeare from such a one-sided and unironic conception of the complexity of human responses to adversity, Shaw must cast it upon 'the workers'. Shaw maintained an un-Marxist intellectual distance from the oppressed, who are merely victims of their circumstances:

Individual slavery is not compatible with that freedom of adventure, that personal refinement and intellectual culture, that scope of action, which the higher and subtler drama demands.... Hamlet's experiences simply could not have happened to a plumber. A poor man is useful on the stage only as a blind man is: to excite sympathy. (Shaw 1972, 289)

Shaw put himself outside the Marxist theatrical and literary tradition that finds in the undiminished spirit of oppressed people exactly 'that freedom of adventure' he denies could survive there. If, as Shaw thought, the Elizabethan mind-set was necessarily closed to ideas whose time had not come—if the range of ideas that may be thought is entirely constrained by economic reality and the superstructure merely reflects the base—there is no accounting for historical change and no point 'dreaming on things to come'. Getting there from here sometimes means breaking our habits of representation, but Shaw was essentially conservative about this; responding to an enquiry about the art of stage performance he wrote that 'The beginning and end of the business from the author's point of view is the art of making the audience believe that real things are happening to real people' (Shaw 1958, 153). There are, in fact, other more radical ways to theorize theatre.

Bertolt Brecht's Marxism and Shakespeare

Shaw's *Saint Joan* was produced by Max Reinhardt at the Deutsches Theater in Berlin in 1924, and attending the rehearsals was the 26-year-old assistant dramaturg Bertolt Brecht whose first play, *Baal*, had premiered the previous year. Brecht had not studied Marx when he published his 'Three Cheers for Shaw' in the *Berliner Börsen-Courier* on 25 July 1926, but he leavened his admiration with correction:

He [Shaw] said that in future people would no longer go to the theatre in order to understand something. What he probably meant was that, odd as it may seem, the mere reproduction of reality does not give an impression of truth. If so the younger generation will not contradict him; but I must point out that the reason why Shaw's own dramatic works dwarf those of his contemporaries is that they so unhesitatingly appealed to the reason. His world is one that arises from opinions. (Brecht 1964, 11)

The term 'Brechtian' is now commonly applied to almost any kind of surprising theatrical device, but the essence of Brecht's thinking was this appeal to the rational over the emotional, and his later accommodations of realism were nonetheless in the service of reason.

Brecht's famous dramatic principle of alienation was not the Marxist one we met in Chapter 1, but something closer to ideas emerging in the Russian Formalism of the Moscow Linguistic Circle founded in 1915 and Viktor Shklovsky's Society for the Study of Poetic Language founded in Petrograd in 1916. The Russian Formalists set out to answer the question 'What is literariness?', bearing in mind that literature is made out of the same raw material, words, that we use to write shopping lists and discuss the weather. They decided that literariness is the selection of words not for their content but for their form, such as having endings of the same sound (rhyme), having stresses that fall into a regular beat (rhythm), or being placed in an order that defers the main verb until the end of a sentence (syntax). All literary devices do this 'organized violence' (as Roman Jakobson later called it) to ordinary speech in order to recover its strangeness, to 'defamiliarize' or 'make strange' language in order that we may see afresh the everyday world that is encoded in familiar words. By focusing not on what is said but on the way it is said, literature shakes us out of habitual thinking and makes us regard everyday normality with a fresh eye. For Stalin, the Russian Formalists' insistence on the medium not the message was a dangerous bourgeois distraction from exhorting workers to ever greater heroism for the sake of increased production; the movement was suppressed in the late 1920s and Socialist Realism became the official Soviet aesthetic in all the arts.

How much Brecht demurred from Shaw's concern for 'making the audience believe that real things are happening to real people' is clear in his essay 'The Street Scene: A Basic Model for an Epic Theatre' (Brecht 1964, 121–9). Imagine a street corner, Brecht began, just after a road traffic accident, where an eyewitness explains the events to bystanders. To illustrate, the eyewitness might impersonate the driver being distracted by his girlfriend in the next seat, or the peculiar walk of the victim; an illusion of reality is not the point:

Suppose he cannot carry out some particular movement as quickly as the victim he is imitating; all he need do is explain that *he* moves three times as fast, and the demonstration neither suffers in essentials nor loses its point. On the contrary it is important that he should not be too perfect. His demonstration would be spoilt if the bystanders' attention were drawn to his powers of transformation. He has to avoid presenting himself in such a way that someone calls out 'What a lifelike portrayal of a chauffeur!' He must not 'cast a spell' over anyone. . . . The demonstration would become no less valid if he did not reproduce the fear caused by the accident; on the contrary it would lose validity if he did. He is not interested in creating pure emotions. (Brecht 1964, 122)

As a model for theatre this would seem in danger of denying pleasure in order to promote a mind-numbing literalness; as Terry Eagleton remarked, Brecht would presumably have staged *Waiting for Godot* in front of a large banner reading 'He's not going to come, you know' (Eagleton 2001, 70). More Brechtian still might be to have a surprise entrance for Godot 10 minutes in, bringing the play to an early, happy ending.

For Brecht, all theatre should share the social significance of the eyewitness's account—the driver might be fired for negligence, the victim might be permanently disfigured—and in place of Shaw's concern for imitation of objective reality is Brecht's desire to put everything up to purposeful contestation: the driver's tone of voice matters if one may get from it a sense of exasperation about working excessive hours (so the employer is to blame), the victim's umbrella should be mentioned if it obstructed his vision. The actor, like the eyewitness, should remain detached from the performance and not be 'wholly transformed into the person demonstrated', as Stanislavsky taught (Brecht 1964, 125). This detachment gives the performer's art a twofold quality (demonstrator and demonstrated) that, as we shall see in Chapter 3, has been claimed as the principle ('bifold authority') underlying Renaissance dramatic performance.

Brecht's 'alienation' (*verfremdungseffekt*) devices were intended to forestall the collapse of the difference between the role and the performer promoted by realist theatre technologies and conventions. An alienated audience remains alert, rational, and willing to pass judgement rather than being swept away by emotional identification; spectators should retain their everyday approach to representation rather than suspending their disbelief. The Russian Formalists' 'estrangement' (*ostrananie*) devices work the other way; they are what literature does to show how extraordinary are our everyday words and concepts, but the aim is the same: to unsettle unconscious habits of mind. The 'settled state' arises in the first case from theatre's traditions (art strives to the condition of reality) and in the second from our everyday use of language (by familiarity we forget that reality is artfully constructed).

As we saw in Chapter 1, Marxist alienation (*entfremdung*) happens when commodity production takes away the individual characteristic of what is produced, when by reification objects no longer seem shaped by the human labour that formed them but take on a mysterious intangibility beyond the producer's control. Brecht saw something of the same happening in the alienation effects of existing theatrical traditions:

> The classical and medieval theatre alienated its characters by making them wear human or animal masks; the Asiatic theatre even today uses musical and pantomimic A-effects.... The old A-effects quite remove the object represented from the spectator's grasp, turning it into something that cannot be altered; the new are not odd in themselves, though the unscientific eye stamps anything strange as odd. The new alienations are only designed to free socially-conditioned phenomena from the stamp of familiarity which protects them against our grasp today. (Brecht 1964, 192)

Brecht's kind of alienation opposed the mystifying one of commodity production and of traditional theatrical production, and its aim was to expose the contradictions of everyday existence: the potential to express its own opposite that lies latent in every occasion, decision, feeling, description, or action. At any point in a narrative whatever happens next is but one of many possibilities that might have occurred, and Brecht wanted the audience to perceive the many possibilities rejected in taking a particular course, even one as trivial as moving downstage rather than upstage.

The longest, yet still incomplete, explication of Brecht's ideas about drama is *The Messingkauf Dialogues* in which the Dramaturg argues that Naturalism presented images of the world that made audiences critical of the world and so they went and changed it, but the Philosopher responds that Naturalism generated feeble criticism because the audience identified with the world shown them and this weakened their desire to change it: people came to terms with the world as represented. The world and its people have been forever changing, and it is immutability, not change, that we should see as small-minded:

Miserable philistines will always find the same motive forces in history, their own. Man with a capital M drinks coffee every afternoon, is jealous of his wife, wants to get on in the world, and only more or less manages to: more often less. 'People don't change much,' he says.... Anything can happen to him; he's at home in any disaster. He has been rewarded with ingratitude like *Lear*, been enraged like *Richard III*. He has given up everything for his wife, like *Antony* did for Cleopatra, and has nagged her more or less as *Othello* did his. He is as hesitant as *Hamlet* to right a wrong by bloodshed; his friend's are like *Timon*'s. (Brecht 1965, 48)

The idea, of course, is not that Shakespeare's plays are so small in their concerns, but that the bourgeois mind finds in them analogies for its own small concerns, and thus the drama swells their sense of importance; what one should get from them is a sense of historical determinants and change.

For Brecht Shakespeare's works in their original performance context were radically non-realistic:

[THE DRAMATURG:] *Richard III* Act V scene 3 shows two camps with the tents of Richard and Richmond and in between these a ghost appearing in a dream to the two men, visible and audible to each of them and addressing itself to both. A theatre full of A-effects!... Add to that the fact that they acted (and also rehearsed, of course) by daylight in the open air, mostly without any attempt to indicate the place of the action and in the closest proximity to the audience, who sat on all sides, including the stage, with a crowd standing or strolling around, and you'll begin to get an idea how earthly, profane and lacking in magic it all was. (Brecht 1965, 58–9)

Shaw's non-Marxist historical sense could provide no explanation for Shakespeare's greatness other than his possession of a musical way with words that made beautiful the 'platitudes of proverbial philosophy'. However, Brecht saw Shakespeare occupying a unique historical moment, the juncture of the late feudal and early capitalist ages and managing to get something of the contradiction between the two into his plays.

Marx's historical materialism sees the increasing forces of production as the engine of change that first breaks through the fetters of the old system that is holding it back and forces the transition to a new system in which production is liberated, only for the new system to itself become a fetter on the restlessly advancing capacity of human beings to make things. For Brecht this was the origin of Shakespearian tragedy:

THE PHILOSOPHER: He takes a tragic view of the decline of feudalism. *Lear,*
tied up in his own patriarchal ideas; *Richard III,* the unlikeable man who
makes himself terrifying; *Macbeth,* the ambitious man swindled by witches;
Antony, the hedonist who hazards his mastery of the world; *Othello,* destroyed by jealousy: they are all living in a new world and are smashed by
it.... [H]ow could there be anything more complex, fascinating and important than the decline of great ruling classes? (Brecht 1965, 59)

Thus there is a great difference between our historical moment and
Shakespeare's, and yet there is an essential parallel too, for being
(hopefully) near the end of the capitalist era we are likewise 'fathers
of a new period and sons of an old one' and 'What really matters is to
play these old works historically, which means setting them in powerful contrast to our own time' (Brecht 1965, 63–4).

World Pictures: Dialecticism, Soviet and Elizabethan

In dealing with the tricky matter of how far consciousness is shaped by
social being, how much the superstructure is determined by the economic base, Marxists often avoid giving a straight answer by drawing
upon a philosophical means of having one's cake and eating it too
called the dialectic. The art of dialectic derives its name from philosophical dialogue, the exploration by debate between speakers taking
opposed positions, from which back-and-forth disputation emerges a
new product, truth. In the course of mocking P. J. Proudhon's use
of dialectic, Marx gave his version of Hegel's philosophical abstraction that sought to find the source of the universal principle of
movement:

What is movement in abstract condition? The purely logical formula of
movement or the movement of pure reason. Wherein does the movement of
pure reason consist? In posing itself, opposing itself, composing itself; in
formulating itself as thesis, antithesis, synthesis; or, yet, in affirming itself,
negating itself and negating its negation.... But once it has managed to pose
itself as a thesis, this thesis, this thought, opposed to itself, splits up into two
contradictory thoughts—the positive and the negative, the yes and no. The
struggle between these two antagonistic elements comprised in the antithesis
constitutes the dialectical movement. The yes becoming no, the no becoming
yes, the yes becoming both yes and no, the no becoming both no and yes, the
contraries balance, neutralize, paralyze each other. The fusion of these two
contradictory thoughts constitutes a new thought, which is the synthesis of

them. This thought splits up once again into two contradictory thoughts, which in turn fuse into a new synthesis. (Marx [1935], 90–1)

Where Marx differed from Hegel was in placing reality before ideas, so that this principle of self-contradiction and progress inheres in the material world *before* (and not as consequence of) its operation in Hegel's bodiless World Spirit or Idea. If a Marxist sounds like she is contradicting herself, she has the ready excuse that that is the nature of the world.

As a theory of knowledge, the Marxist dialectic opposes Idealism in its subjective form (the view that we can only know sensory experiences, not the objects that give rise to them) and its objective form (the view that we can know reality by pure intuition). Where Proudhon went wrong was to stop after the first binary split, say the good and bad aspects of the division of labour, and seek a synthesis there, such as finding a way to keep the good aspects and overcome the bad. As Marx wittily put it, Proudhon could not 'raise himself above the first two rungs of simple thesis and antithesis; and even these he has mounted only twice, and on one of these two occasions he fell over backwards' (Marx [1935], 92).

The relationship between ideas and reality is something Shakespeare's Richard II reflects upon in prison, and although couched in biological language his soliloquy has all the necessary elements— synthesis of opposites, self-negation, progression—of the Hegelian dialectic:

> Yet I'll hammer it out.
> My brain I'll prove the female to my soul,
> My soul the father, and these two beget
> A generation of still-breeding thoughts;
> And these same thoughts people this little world
> In humours like the people of this world.
> For no thought is contented. The better sort,
> As thoughts of things divine, are intermixed
> With scruples, and do set the faith itself
> Against the faith
>
> (5.5.5–14)

Richard finds that physical reality is primary:

Thoughts tending to ambition, they do plot
Unlikely wonders: how these vain weak nails
May tear a passage through the flinty ribs
Of this hard world, my ragged prison walls;
And for they cannot, die in their own pride.

(5.5.18–22)

In this apparently static mode of self-contemplation, Richard reports that his thoughts are utterly constrained: some die seeking to transcend their material circumstances, others (those 'tending to content') give a little ease at the cost of quietism. Marx believed that human consciousness inevitably undertook self-examination in which it was both subject and object, and that this was an engine of intellectual progression because self-knowledge changes the subject, and hence the object, of the examination. Among the new thoughts that Richard's mind begets is the one that he has been thinking about his different kinds of thoughts as though they were people, and this thought is unlike the others for it is articulated in the moment as his soliloquy. To articulate this thought, time runs backwards as the speech moves from a future ('I'll hammer it out') to the present tense ('Thoughts . . . die') and yet also forward from the creation of the thoughts to their demise.

Such a forward-and-backward tension exists in a scripted speech that an actor must make seem like spontaneous thought, and in certain kinds of musical performance. Jazz pianist Art Tatum claimed that 'There's no such thing as a wrong note, it all depends on how you resolve it' (Monk 1972), meaning that the correctness of a musical phrase can only be determined retrospectively; from a perspective subsequently available the spontaneous act can be seen to take on a purpose. When out-of-time music plays (5.5.41) Richard is struck first by its discordance and then by the concordance between this discord and his own disorderly past; it is dialectically discordant and concordant all at once. The Marxist sense of history has this tension between inevitability and spontaneity, for historical materialism insists that the transitions from feudalism to capitalism to communism follow iron laws created by increasing forces of production, and yet Marx exhorted the workers of the world to bring about the change. Can freely chosen actions by people be also the working out of a predestined history?

This is essentially also the Christian paradox that freely willed human choices are already factored into the divine plan, and in that form Shakespeare repeatedly confronted it.

Richard's thoughts are in his head, and are as confined there as he is in prison. However, that prison exists only in the minds of the audience, for he stands on the same stage where just 50 lines earlier (perhaps two or three minutes of stage time) the Duchess of Gloucester pleaded for her son's life and complained that her husband set 'the word itself against the word' (5.3.120). Indeed, it seems that Shakespeare originally had Richard use this phrase too, and changed it to 'faith itself against the faith' as quoted above to avoid repeating himself (Wells et al. 1987, 313). The productive self-contradictoriness of language (word against word) arises from the self-contradictoriness of consciousness, for the act of self-reflection (the hallmark of consciousness) changes what it examines as it examines it. We can report to ourselves only what we were, not what we are, since what we are is changed by the reporting and becomes something new—we become the people who know what they were—and this process runs ahead of all further reporting.

The dialectic between object and subject—self-knowledge forever transforming one into the other—is equally the dialectic between base and superstructure, for part of the superstructure is the self-examination of society that Marxism (and other progressive movements) undertakes and that in this moment changes what is observed. As we saw in Chapter 1, Georg Lukács made this point in his *History and Class Consciousness* (in German, 1923) that gave a special place to proletarian class consciousness, which, once sufficiently universal, transmutates from subjectivity into objectivity. Human consciousness is ahead of social being, informed by knowledge of economic reality and forever pushed forward by ongoing recognition of that reality; this is a mutually sustaining form of progression that locks social being and consciousness together and that can be understood without notions of mechanical determination or of ideas mirroring reality.

In the late 1930s Stalin used Hegel's dialectic and Marx's historical materialism to create dialectical materialism, which he made the official philosophy of Marxist-Leninism, itself the official doctrine of the Soviet communist countries. Neither Marx nor Lenin would have agreed to a single philosophical principle underpinning everything from political progress to the geophysical sciences. One of

Stalin's memorable images for dialectics in practice was the way that the back-and-forth motion of pistons in an internal combustion engine is converted to a linear force pushing the vehicle forward, and such transformatory machines themselves were central to the Soviet Five Year Plan of 1929 and its successors: progress would literally be driven by the increasing forces of production. A symmetrical counterpart to the dialectic's transformation of the reciprocal jerks into forward progress was the principle of quantity forever transforming into quality, so that the smoothly increasing quantity of productive power results in a series of qualitatively distinct epochs of slavery, feudalism, capitalism, and socialism.

In 1937, just as dialectical materialism became the official Soviet template for thinking about everything in general, and Socialist Realism was confirmed as the template for creating art, there appeared in London three books of Marxist literary criticism that posited an utterly mechanical connection between base and superstructure, reading literary epochs and genres as mere projections of prevailing economic conditions: Christopher Caudwell's *Illusion and Reality*, Alick West's *Crisis and Criticism*, and Ralph Fox's *The Novel and the People*. Although Caudwell insisted on the need to understand modern poetry 'historically—in motion', he quoted *The Communist Manifesto*'s famous passage about the bourgeoisie's perpetual revolutionizing of the means of production: 'All that is solid melts into air'. (This is Caudwell's, and the famous, phrasing. An alternative translation is 'All that is privileged and established melts into air' (Marx and Engels 1948, 17).) Caudwell concluded that

Capitalist poetry reflects these conditions. It is the outcome of these conditions. . . . Its art is therefore in its essence an insurgent, non-formal, naturalistic art. . . . It is an art which constantly revolutionizes its own conventions, just as bourgeois economy constantly revolutionises its own means of production (Caudwell 1937, 53, 55).

Caudwell's mechanical view of determination was clear in such assertions as 'All men's minds are distorted by bourgeois presuppositions through living in a bourgeois economy' (Caudwell 1937, 311).

Caudwell was in Spain preparing to fight the Fascists when *Illusion and Reality* appeared, and he was killed giving covering machine-gun fire to his comrades on his first day of action. Two more books were sufficiently complete for almost immediate posthumous publication, *Studies in a Dying Culture* (1938) and *The Crisis in Physics* (1939), and they show the trend of Caudwell's mechanist thinking. All aspects of bourgeois culture, including its hard and soft sciences, the psychological theories of Freud, and the economic theories of Keynes, were to Caudwell inherently polluted by the distance that the intellectual class kept from the working class. Einsteinian relativity Caudwell saw as a necessarily vain attempt to ameliorate the superstructural incoherence that the capitalist base was bound to generate, and he looked forward to the arrival of a single Marxist *Weltanschauung* that would unite the fissiparous strands of intellectual life. It is unlikely that Caudwell would have accepted Stalin's form of a singular approach to art and science, but his thinking tended the same way in its rejection of the (objectively true) scientific ideas that emerged under capitalism.

Alick West also saw art as an objective manifestation of a particular set of economic arrangements, and denied the place of any kind of relativism in literary judgments:

Marx said that a railway is only potentially a railway if nobody travels on it. In the same way, it may be said that Shakespeare is only potentially Shakespeare if nobody reads him with appreciation. But the act of appreciation no more creates his valuable work than the travelling on the railway creates the railway. The statement that value is a mere elevation of popularity into the absolute, leads to the position that we create our own Shakespeares. (West 1937, 135–6)

As we shall see in Chapter 3, one strand of Marxist thinking has led to the recent insistence upon what West saw as absurd: that we do indeed create our own Shakespeares in our acts of interpretation. For West, Shakespeare's greatness is historical in the sense that he aligned himself with what was progressive in his age, and James Joyce's *Ulysses* fails because he 'cannot identify himself with any particular phase of social movement. . . . Consequently the book does not organise social energy; it irritates it, because it gives it no aim it can work for' (West 1937, 179–80).

Unsurprisingly, in this pragmatic approach the duality of form and content is not an equality, or even a dialectic, but a hierarchy, so that 'content is of prior importance' (West 1937, 131) and form limps after:

This, of course, does not mean that the particular decision represented by the content of Shakespeare's sonnet determines its sonnet form; but it modifies the previously existing sonnet form. And the form which Shakespeare finds ready to his hand is itself the result of an endless number of new contents slightly modifying the form in which previous contents had been embodied. In this sense, content, the particular action, determines form, the result of previous action. (West 1937, 132)

Ralph Fox might almost have been thinking of West's comment that '. . . the tendency of capitalism is to frustrate and of socialism to develop literature' (West 1937, 181–2) when he distanced his Marxism from the 'crude and vulgar' view that because 'the capitalist mode of production was a more progressive one than the feudal, capitalist art must therefore always stand on a higher level than feudal art, while feudal art in turn must stand above the art of the slave States of Greece and Rome' (Fox 1937, 19–20). Yet Fox too subordinated form to content, in history and in art:

Marxism . . . while reserving the final and decisive factor in any change for economic causes, does not deny that 'ideal' factors can also influence the course of history and may even preponderate in determining the *form* which changes will take (but only the form). . . . [Marx] understood perfectly well that religion, or philosophy, or tradition can play a great part in the creation of a work of art, even that any one of these or other 'ideal' factors may preponderate in determining the *form* of the work in question. (Fox 1937, 21–2)

Also like West, Fox's sense of history put Shakespeare in the right place at the right time, and he complained that Evelyn Waugh's biography of Edmund Campion was 'crowned with the Hawthornden prize', which shows the bankruptcy of modern criticism:

But would Shakespeare or Marlowe have considered Campion a martyr? Or would they not have inclined to the view that his activities, at a time when England was fighting for national existence, fighting for the conditions which created our national culture, were best characterised by Shakespeare's reference to:

> 'the fools of time,
> Which die for goodness, who have liv'd for crime.' (Fox 1937, 13)

To match Fox's rage his printer appears to have rendered typographically the incoherence of his philistinic view of the causes of the English novel's decline into solipsism: 'Psycho-analysis, as developed by Frued, [sic] is the apotheosis of the individual. the [sic] extreme of intlleectual [sic] anarchy' (Fox 1937, 13).

Fox's prescribed cure was simply '...Marxism with its artistic formula of a "socialist realism" which shall unite and re-vitalise the forces of the Left in literature' (Fox 1937, 15). By this means the missing hero would be restored to the novel, for 'the creation of character' (Fox 1937, 88) is the novel's chief concern, and although he had the misfortune to work in the wrong genre, 'Shakespeare's characters are their [Marx and Engel's] ideal of how the Marxist writer should present man, as being at one and the same time a type and an individual, a representative of the mass and a single personality' (Fox 1937, 108). Judged from these three books of 1937, the future of Marxist literary theorizing looked bleak.

To be fair, however, it was not only the Marxists who explained everything by social pressure, leaving the writer no autonomy, as we can see from the telling subtitle of Lily B. Campbell's *Shakespeare's Histories: Mirrors of Elizabethan Policy* (1947). The most influential Shakespeare critic from the first half of the twentieth century addressed himself squarely to this matter of determination. In *The Elizabethan World Picture* (1943) E. M. W. Tillyard outlined what a typical educated Elizabethan thought about how the world was ordered, the principles of temporal and divine governance, and the relationship between human affairs and the divine scheme. Tillyard saw a general faith in order and stability, manifested in an imagined Great Chain of Being that allocated everything its place in a coherent structure, a hierarchy, that ultimately led to God. From lowest to highest, each element of the universe is linked to the others by this chain and is pulled from above and below. The best aspects of a 'noble' beast are almost as good as, and are being pulled towards, the worst aspects of humanity, while the worst part of it is like a lower animal. The worst part of a lower animal is little better than plant life, and the worst of plant life, moss growing on a rock, is little better than the rock on which it grows; human beings are thus torn between beastliness and the angelic. Social mobility, then, would be as absurd as a carrot wanting to be a rose, or a frog wanting to be a lion. In particular, the monarch was supposed to be God's deputy on earth, the binding link between heavenly and earthly order, and duty to one's monarch was a religious obligation.

Tillyard was immediately accused of over-simplification, of treating art as merely a mirror of politics, of allowing too little room for dissent, and indeed he was guilty, but his was an excusable reaction to the prevailing methodology of New Criticism that denied that context held any critical value. For New Critics, literary works function as public artefacts discovered by examination of their internal features, to be explored

through the semantics and syntax of a poem, through our habitual knowledge of the language, through grammars, dictionaries, and all the literature which is the source of dictionaries, in general through all that makes a language and culture; while what is external is private or idiosyncratic; not a part of the work as a linguistic fact: it consists of revelations (in journals, for example, or letters or reported conversations) about how or why the poet wrote the poem.... (Wimsatt and Beardsley 1946, 477–8)

W. K. Wimsatt and M. C. Beardsley's account seems to have no place for the impersonal, historical pressures that condition any piece of writing, unless we suppose that they have smuggled them in via the phrase 'all that makes a language and culture', which necessarily changes over time. What they explicitly say of the external forces are things about the conscious life of the writer, not the unconscious.

Wimsatt and Beardsley were themselves reacting against a kind of biographical historicism that sought the meaning of writing in the life experiences of the writer and they insisted—in a manner that pre-echoes poststructuralist concerns we will meet in Chapter 4—on the social nature of literature:

The poem is not the critic's own and not the author's (it is detached from the author at birth and goes about the world beyond his power to intend about it or control it). The poem belongs to the public. It is embodied in language, the peculiar possession of the public, and it is about the human being, an object of public knowledge. (Wimsatt and Beardsley 1946, 470)

Here, then, is a symptomatic tension in literary theory, and one that Marxism cannot avoid: in demanding that the work can only be understood in the context of its own consumption—being written for readers or audiences—the critic diminishes the particular historical context (who wrote it, for whom, and how they felt about each other), but rather than making the text stand alone (as certain New Critics hoped) this only serves to embed the work more deeply in the context of a shared language that, as we saw in Chapter 1, encodes particular ways of thinking and feeling about the world.

Although it is universally absent from his detractors' caricatures, Tillyard's model has a contradiction at its heart, between inherited medieval ideas (especially the religious injunction to contemn the world) and the humanism emerging since the twelfth century: 'The two contradictory principles co-existed in a state of high tension' (Tillyard 1943, 2). The World Picture was not monolithic but rather a site of contestation as the work of Machiavelli and Copernicus (Tillyard 1943, 73) provided new reasons to reject traditional ideas and the ruling dynasty sought to marshal ideological support for its own rule: 'Somehow the Tudors had inserted themselves into the constitution of the medieval universe' (Tillyard 1943, 6). The agency of the ruling dynasty and the need for ongoing work to maintain this World Picture makes it much more properly ideological in the senses explored in Chapter 1 than the vulgar understanding of that word available in the work of Caudwell, West, and Fox. An effect of the orthodox scheme of salvation was to polarize dissent: 'You could revolt against it but you could not ignore it. Atheism not agnosticism was the rule' (Tillyard 1943, 16).

In Tillyard's view the tension between the pessimistic *contemptus mundi* and optimistic humanism was a form of dialectic already present in Platonism: the universe is essentially good because it is a copy of God's perfect idea, and the universe is essentially bad because it is only a copy. This tension between competing ideas was irreducible, '. . . there was equal pressure on both sides', and it operated within individuals, who might therefore enjoy a humanistic play and a hell-fire sermon on the same day (Tillyard 1943, 20). What appears to have been most offensive to recent anti-Tillyardians was his model of the Chain of Being stretching 'from the foot of God's throne to the meanest of inanimate objects' (Tillyard 1943, 23). Each item within the chain was necessarily lesser than the one above and greater than the one below, so that relational value is all: rank order marks the differences of things, no two are equal.

The Chain of Being offends modern liberal sensibility that has detached 'difference' from 'inequality' and insisted that all are equal despite their differences; terminologically this separation is recent and has not reached mathematics where these words are synonyms.

Raymond Williams acutely observed that advocates of equality of opportunity, of 'say, wages graduated in proportion to effort' alone, are actually calling for an equal right to become unequal (Williams 1958, 165) and he approvingly quoted D. H. Lawrence's insistence that

One man is neither equal nor unequal to another man. When I stand in the presence of another man, and I am my own pure self, am I aware of the presence of an equal, or of an inferior, or of a superior? I am not.... I am only aware of a Presence, and of the strange reality of Otherness. (Williams 1958, 211)

Williams himself distinguished two kinds of equality, one good and one bad:

The only equality that is important, or indeed conceivable, is equality of being. Inequality in the various aspects of man is inevitable and even welcome; it is the basis of any rich and complex life. The equality that is evil is inequality which denies the essential equality of being. (Williams 1958, 317)

The Chain of Being offers a kind of equality in making all equally part of the God's plan, and 'no part was superfluous' (Tillyard 1943, 28), as is the worker in David Heneker's Second World War song 'The Thing-ummy-bob', sung separately by Gracie Fields and Arthur Askey, about the woman who 'makes the thing that drills the hole that holds the ring... that's going to win the war'.

Tillyard did not leave human agency, especially subversion, out of his model, as is often claimed: it is there, for example, in the stars being supposed intermediaries between Fortune and human affairs, obeying God's changeless order yet responsible for the vagaries of luck in the sublunar realm. This would seem a pessimistic view of things, and hence one serving conservatism, had not Tillyard insisted that '... the prevalence of the doctrine... that the stars' influence can be resisted may not be sufficiently recognized' and hence, although Tillyard did not use this example, Romeo's 'I defy you, stars' (5.1.24) is not merely adolescent bravado (Tillyard 1943, 53, 55). As James L. Calderwood noted, stars were also the means by which mariners plotted their own courses so there too is a dialectical confluence of dependence and autonomy (Calderwood 1971, 115n13).

Characters in Renaissance drama explain their misfortunes in astro-logical terms, but Tillyard likened the difference between medieval astrology and its Elizabethan descendant to the difference between 'real' (that is, 'royal') tennis and its later variant (Tillyard 1943, 49). The appositeness of his analogy is not made explicit by Tillyard—a recurrent failing that caused much misunderstanding of this book—for the reciprocal and unpredictable movement of tennis balls is one of the most common images used by Renaissance dramatic characters for the vagaries of human existence, extending even into the titles of Middleton's *The World Tossed at Tennis* and Dekker's *Fortune's Tennis*, and even when tennis is not mentioned it can be an underlying metaphor (Hopkins 2000).

The bandied tennis ball appealed to Elizabethans as a metaphor for the unpredictability of human existence just as the jerks of microscopic particles subject to Brownian motion appealed to the Modernists and to Futurists such as Filippo Marinetti (Marinetti 1913). However, whereas Brownian motion actually is random, a tennis ball's motion is subject to deterministic physical laws as well as the rules of the game, and ultimately is governed by creatures (the players) who are not the ball's peers and whose ends the balls serve. As Brecht observed, 'It is scarcely possible to conceive of the laws of motion if one looks at them from a tennis ball's point of view' (Brecht 1964, 275), so one needs to adopt the right frame of reference. That characters in Renaissance drama liken themselves to tennis balls does not mean that the Elizabethans thought that the forces acting upon us are unknowable, nor that the universe is chaotic, only that the plays expose the experience of being subject to laws that, as Brecht always insisted, the audience might well be able to understand even as the characters fail to.

Tillyard thought that the World Picture he described was under attack in Shakespeare's time, and as its tidy categories increasingly failed to fit reality the 'equivalences shaded off into resemblances'; nonetheless the model was used 'to tame a bursting and pullulating world' (Tillyard 1943, 93). The strongest pressure came from newer truths: Copernican astronomy 'had by then broken the fiction of the eternal and immutable heavens' (Tillyard 1943, 99). This sense that the World Picture was part of intellectual equipment with which one might make sense of a rapidly changing, confusing early modern world is unavailable in the characterizations of Tillyard's detractors, who often seem to think that Tillyard himself believed in the World Picture.

Far from identifying himself with his model, Tillyard characterized its ideas as 'very queer' and, in an oblique reference to 'certain trends of thought in central Europe', compared its strangeness to Nazism and Fascism. Just because these things strike us as crazy is no reason to ignore them, as 'scientifically minded intellectuals' have tended to do (Tillyard 1943, 101–2). Tillyard insisted on the World Picture as ideology put to work 'by the Tudor regime', and like Shaw (pp. 46–50 above) he thought Shakespeare's genius lay in dressing with beautiful language 'the common property of every thirdrate mind of the age' (Tillyard 1943, 100–1). Reviewing the book, Don Cameron Allen misunderstood Tillyard to say that the Elizabethans' ideas were not queer and, although he thought the picture partial, praised Tillyard for 'an immense service in reducing a certain point of view to its minimum essentials'. Writing about the anti-Tillyardism of New Historicism and Cultural Materialism, Graham Bradshaw called Allen's review of Tillyard's book 'devastating' (Bradshaw 1993, 3), which is hardly the right word for its faint praise.

Tillyard's next book, *Shakespeare's History Plays* (1944), argued that a model of divine Providence governed Elizabethans' feelings about the deposition of Richard II (a great sin) and so the ensuing civil war (in the Henry IV, Henry V, and Henry VI plays) would have been understood as divine retribution necessary before the return of order in Henry VII's reign. This book too, and for good reason, was accused of homogenizing Elizabethan views of historical change, as when Geoffrey Tillotson complained that Tillyard 'has become interested in certain notions of theirs, and he tends to think of them as repositories of those notions' (Tillotson 1945, 160). In particular, Tillyard failed to spot that, like Shakespeare's plays, the chronicle sources offer multiple explanations and points of view rather than a single providential account of history (Kelly 1970). Attacking Tillyard became a specialist sub-domain of critical activity, and Bradshaw and Robin Headlam Wells were moved by the second wave of anti-Tillyardians' ignorance of the first. Wells drew attention to A. P. Rossiter's early rejection of Tillyardian 'certainty and moral conviction' in favour of 'ambivalence' and Rossiter's claim that Shakespeare's history plays show 'mutually opposed points of view both of which seem equally valid' (Wells 1985, 398).

Wells approvingly quoted critics who thought Tillyard overlooked the 'unresolved dialectic' in Shakespeare's dramatization of history, his ability to allow 'antithetical meanings to exist concurrently', and the 'purposeful ambiguity' rightly found in Shakespeare 'opposed elements [presented] as equally valid, equally desirable, and equally destructive, so that the choice that the play forces the reader to make becomes impossible' (Wells 1985, 399). Wells closed with the view of 'exceptionally shrewd' W. R. Elton that Shakespeare plays give us 'an appropriate conflictual structure: a dialectic of ironies and ambivalences, avoiding in its complex movement and dialogue the simplifications of direct statement and reductive resolution' (Wells 1985, 403).

This is the Marxist terminology of dialectic and conflict co-opted to a liberal-conservative agenda, for an 'unresolved dialectic' is in fact no dialectic at all. The essence of dialecticism is progress by transcendence achieved in conflict, but Wells was captivated by the very impossibility of resolution, by the paralysis engendered of mutually opposed ideas locked in a deadly embrace of perfectly equal intellectual force. This is the characteristic liberal view, perceiving the world's problems but finding the objections to the solution to be equally counterpoised in strength and number so that, ultimately, nothing can be done. This view lacks the faith of the Marxist dialectic (and the Hegelian too) in the potential for progress, but it should not be a reason for Marxists to distance themselves from liberals, as many have done in the past 20 years. Rather, the task is to convince liberals (who have already come half way in agreeing about the problems) to overcome their qualms and join in progressive politics and scholarship.

3

Marx's Influence on Shakespeare Studies since 1968

Between 1937 and 1955 the social research organization Mass-Observation formed by Tom Harrison, Charles Madge, and Humphrey Jennings produced over 3,000 reports on the everyday lives of ordinary people in Britain. After the Second World War, increased access to university education by working-class students generated scholarly works of Marxist history, most notably E. P. Thompson's *The Making of the English Working Class* (1963), that encouraged a 'grass-roots' view of history. In the reformist socialist climate of post-war Britain, working-class life became a subject of reputable academic study and Thompson claimed that English working-class consciousness had itself been forged in the nineteenth century by the courageous deeds of particular activists rather than being the necessary outcome of increasing industrialization. Thompson differed from the Marxists who saw inevitable forces at work in the formation (and triumph) of the working class, and in emphasizing that class's particular achievements he resisted the patronizing caricatures of working-class life that came from liberal and from left-wing positions such as G. B. Shaw's.

Mass-Observation provided raw data for new social history studies of women's lives, and in the 1960s women's raised consciousness generated political demands. How politics and literary criticism coincided in the rise of feminist Shakespeare studies is worth examining in detail because in the developing debates a Marxist understanding of the ways that ideas and representations relate to political practice and real life was repeatedly tested and refined. Several of the central figures would not identify themselves as Marxists and a few well-known

Marxists do not appear in this account because their work did not shape the creation of this new kind of criticism. The aim here is not to give a history of Shakespeare studies generally but to trace the progression of ideas that originate with Marx, and for that reason there is little to say about the period after the mid-1980s. In political practice, everything changed with the collapse of the communist states in 1989–90, and Marxist theory has yet to produce any coherent response to this that might illuminate Shakespeare studies. Dissenting politics flourished in the 1990s, especially in the fields of anarchism, anti-capitalism, animal rights, and ecology, but these are only now beginning to produce new cultural theory.

Feminist Shakespeare studies began with Juliet Dusinberre's *Shakespeare and the Nature of Women* (1975), which argued that the drama is 'feminist in sympathy' (Dusinberre 1975, 5) when Shakespeare puts himself into the minds of his female characters; critical practice can learn from this to take up the female perspective. The editors' programmatic introduction to a collection of essays called *The Woman's Part: Feminist Criticism of Shakespeare* (Lenz, Greene, and Neely 1980b) explicitly called for such a perspective from which to 'see and celebrate his works afresh' (Lenz, Greene, and Neely 1980a, 3). By reading Shakespeare's women without the inherited stereotypes of traditional criticism and within an 'avowedly partisan' (Lenz et al. 1980a, 12) programme of social action, criticism can help the cause of female emancipation. Two contributors to the collection were men yet not excluded from feminist criticism, which 'begins with an individual reader, usually, although not necessarily, a female reader... who brings to the plays her own experience, concerns, questions' (Lenz et al. 1980a, 3). The introduction cautiously hinted at an anti-essentialism that has since become dominant: '...feminine characteristics, like masculine ones, are changing cultural constructs and are not limited to females' (Lenz et al. 1980a, 12).

Linda Bamber began her *Comic Women, Tragic Men* (1982) by rejecting the growing trend to find in Shakespeare the feminist perspectives that criticism had recently taken up; Bamber insisted on 'Shakespeare's indifference to, independence of, and distance from' feminist ideas (Bamber 1982, 2). Where Lenz et al. diminished the importance of the reader/writer's gender, Bamber thought that 'Men must write as men and women as women' and yet '...male or female chauvinism is a separate issue' (Bamber 1982, 5). What matters is whether the writer gives the proper privileges to the characters of the opposite gender (the other) to his or her own (the self), and Shakespeare, she claimed, often does. Shakespeare can be affiliated to the feminist movement 'because in every genre except history he associates the feminine with whatever it is outside himself he takes most seriously' (Bamber 1982, 6). The four-term homology of Bamber's title and the fixity of her self/other distinction ('I presume that heterosexuality will always involve the projection of Otherness onto the opposite sex...' Bamber 1982, 10) show the structuralist ideas in her book, as we shall see, but structure does not imply stasis since as more women write and assume positions of power, 'More and more authors will thus be projecting their sense of Otherness onto men, not women, and the score will begin to even up' (Bamber 1982, 11). Structuralism and responses to it have dominated literary studies since the 1950s, and to see the part that Marxist ideas have played in this process we must return to a revolutionary spring.

Structuralism to Poststructuralism: 1968

In spring 1968, students in the Department of Social Psychology at the University of Nanterre, Paris, produced a pamphlet asking the pertinent question 'Why do we need sociologists?' and supplying their answer: to minimize the social contradictions of capitalism. No discipline reflects so frequently and deeply on itself as literary studies, probably because no one has produced a satisfactory definition of what literature is in the first place. The Russian Formalists' answer—that it is organized violence done to everyday language to defamiliarize it—turned into a theory of breathtaking complexity.

Russian Formalist Roman Jakobson arrived in America in 1941 and taught linguistics, first at Columbia University and then at Harvard. Jakobson's linguistics built upon Ferdinand de Saussure's work on the binary structures that form the distinctions (whether consonantal or not, voiced or not, nasal or not) that allow classification of the smallest unit of sound that can bear such a contrast, the phoneme. The linguist's purview normally ends with the sentence, leaving larger units of writing or speaking such as the paragraph, stanza, scene, or chapter to others, but visiting New York in the early 1940s the French anthropologist Claude Lévi-Strauss saw a way to adapt Jakobson's structural linguistics to the study of kinship systems and of myths, described in his *The Elementary Structures of Kinship* (in French, 1949) and his four-volume series *Mythologiques* (in French, 1964–71). Just as Saussure saw language operating by distinction between minimal units that can be combined to make meaning-bearing structures (words, clauses, sentences) so Jakobson saw myths as being made of 'mythemes', for the meaningful combination of which there was, like language, a set of rules, a grammar.

In his book *Morphology of the Folktale* (in Russian, 1928), Russian Formalist Vladimir Propp identified 31 storytelling units from which all folktales in all cultures are constructed, the 14th of which is 'The hero acquires the use of a magical thing or power' and the 15th 'The hero is transferred, delivered, or led to the place where the thing which he seeks is to be found (often in a strange or foreign place)'. The numbers were ordinal: although not all 31 elements appear in every folktale, those present always appear in numerical order although subplots may be launched with their own sub-sequences. Propp's bold systematizing of the seemingly chaotic phenomenon of folktale works well on other stories too—the film *Star Wars* for example—but is far from a universal theory and for certain applications one must stretch the meanings of the terms considerably to achieve any accord with the story.

Such structuralist analysis (as it came to be known) is founded on the unit called the binary opposition, such as 'culture versus nature' or 'man versus woman', and the simplest structure that can be made is a four-term homology such as 'culture is to nature as man is to woman' or, to take Bamber's example, 'tragedy is to comedy as man is to woman'. Literary studies since the 1960s has been essentially a reaction to structuralism and at the start of the twenty-first century we are still in a poststructuralist phase. Structuralism permeated even where theory was not obviously at work, so that Emrys Jones's *Scenic Form in Shakespeare* (1971) began with the claim that *Macbeth* retains its power even in a Japanese film version because of 'its basic structural shaping: that formal idea which gives the scene its dramatic unity' and just as language has its phoneme and the folktale its mytheme, so '. . . the scene is the primary dramatic unit' (Jones 1971, 3).

A correlative of the structuralist view of language and literature was that order exists in language and in storytelling as extra-personal structures that, as it were, speak through us in individual utterances and texts, or as Lévi-Strauss put it, 'I thus do not aim to show how men think in myths but how myths think in men, unbeknownst to them' (Lévi-Strauss 1970, 20). Where this was acknowledged by structuralists, the determining systems of language and culture tended to be characterized as transhistorical rather than as specific configurations existing at a particular moment within systems that are forever changing. That is to say, while structuralism could in principle support diachronic as well as synchronic analysis, its adherents tended to concentrate on the latter, treating the text as an intricate structure of self-related features that could be studied without recourse to the world of the writer or the particular circumstances of the reader; in its worst excesses structuralism implied that the signifying structures that made Shakespeare intelligible to his first audiences exist unchanged for us.

Saussurian linguistics underlay all these critical developments, and literary scholars continued in apparent ignorance of the linguists' rejection of Saussure that followed the announcement of Noam Chomsky's transformational-generative grammar in *Syntactic Structures* (1957). For Saussure a sentence is a blank template into which the speaker slots particular choices from a range of words, so that the slot for the object of 'The cat sat on the —— ' may be filled with any concrete noun. Chomsky pointed out that 'easy' and 'eager' are equally available to fill the adjective slot in 'Sammy is —— to please'; yet the two resulting sentences differ in the implied object of the verb 'to please', in the first case being Sammy and in the second others. A slot-filling model of grammar overlooks how the particular choices for one slot may affect the senses available for another.

However, when structuralism was first attacked in the late 1960s, it was not for its origin in bad linguistics but for its unit, the binary opposition. What if reality does not divide into tidy categories of opposites, but rather was full of shades of grey in between them? In *Of Grammatology* (in French, 1967) Jacques Derrida pointed out that in such oppositions as day/night, man/woman, white/black, and reason/madness, the positive term can only be defined by negation of its opposite, upon which it thereby depends for its meaning. Countering the centrifugal force pushing the two poles of the opposition apart is a centripetal force of mutual dependence binding them together. Worse still, the two terms often have much in common. The word 'black' comes from the Old Teutonic word 'blækan' meaning to scorch, as does the word 'bleach', because an object placed in a fire turns first black and then, after a while, white. So 'bleaching' (making white) and 'blackening', far from being natural opposites, are cognate. Our binary opposition, which Derrida would say is just a social construct not an adequate description of reality, has just deconstructed itself.

Meaning is only possible when we ignore the inherent self-contradictoriness of our constructs, pretending that we do not see the trace of its own opposite that every utterance contains within it. Derrida explored the binary opposition speaking/writing and the way that Western philosophy has long privileged the first term over the second; doctorates of philosophy are still awarded only on completion of an examination *viva voce*, 'by the living voice'. The voice lives because, until the invention of sound recording, speech guaranteed that the originator of the words was physically present; writing by contrast can travel unaccompanied and cannot be compelled to give an account of itself.

Derrida worked backwards from the speech-centred linguistics of Saussure to Jean-Jacques Rousseau to argue that the entire Western intellectual and philosophical tradition is imbued with phono-centrism:

Saussure takes up the traditional definition of writing which, already in Plato and Aristotle, was restricted to the model of phonetic script and the language of words. Let us recall the Aristotelian definition: 'Spoken words are the symbols of mental experience and written words are the symbols of spoken words.' Saussure: 'Language and writing are two distinct systems of signs; the second *exists for the sole purpose of representing the first*' (p. 45; italics added) [p. 23].... To be sure this factum of phonetic writing is massive; it commands our entire culture and our entire science, and it is certainly not just one fact among others. Nevertheless it does not respond to any necessity of an absolute and universal essence. (Derrida 1976, 30–1)

In Shakespeare's time Philip Sidney offered an audacious challenge to the Platonic tripartite sequential relation of diminishing authenticity of Form, Real-Instance, Artistic-Copy, by arguing that art could reach a perfection not available in reality: 'Nature['s] ... world is brazen, the poets only deliver a golden' (Sidney 1965, 100). Derrida made a parallel argument to disrupt the Platonic sequence of diminishing authenticity of Thought, Speech, Writing, by arguing that the instability of writing is already inside speech and indeed thought, or rather that the inside/outside binary is misleading: 'Il n'y a pas de hors-texte', 'there is nothing outside the text' (Derrida 1976, 158).

As Derrida's work was being consumed by its first readers, France was convulsed by workers' strikes, protests against the Vietnam War, and militant student action. Overcrowded student accommodation was common, especially at the University of Nanterre in Paris, which was taken over by its students in March 1968 who began to produce leaflets calling into question the purpose of their studies. In early May a delegation from Nanterre arrived at the Sorbonne, where student activists joined with those (including staff) about to be disciplined for the takeover at Nanterre. The Sorbonne authorities called in the Compagnies Républicaines de Sécurité (CRS riot police) and closed the university. Weeks of barricade building and sporadic fighting between police and the students (supported by other striking workers) followed, during which the Sorbonne and the École de Beaux-Arts were occupied, and a wave of strikes shut down industrial Normandy, Paris, and Lyons. Soon 12 million French workers were on strike and on 24 May the Paris Stock Exchange was set alight.

In Vietnam, the Tet Offensive convinced the American government to open the negotiations that would eventually lead to its withdrawal, and the reformist Czechoslovakian government of Alexander Dubcek announced its Action Programme that included autonomy for Slovaks, a constitution guaranteeing civil rights, executive power given to a National Assembly, and an independent judiciary, all amounting to what Dubcek called 'socialism with a human face'. The Northern Ireland Civil Rights Association (NICRA), formed in 1967, was modelled on the American Civil Rights movement and sought to bring universal suffrage to a part of the United Kingdom that still withheld the vote from those (mostly Catholic) who did not own property and gave multiple votes to those (mostly Protestant) who owned properties and businesses. A peaceful NICRA march on 5 October 1968 in Derry, attended by three British Labour Party members of parliament and a television crew from the Irish Republic, was broken up by the Royal Ulster Constabulary baton-charging the crowd, and when film of this was shown around the world, international public interest was turned upon the statelet. The continued domination by Unionists of the local government of Derry, a city with a substantial Catholic majority, led to insurrection and the formation of Free Derry, an autonomous Catholic enclave from which the Protestant-dominated police and the British army were excluded.

Nineteen sixty-eight was a momentous year for emancipatory struggles, but they all failed. De Gaulle's government promised a one-third increase in the minimum industrial wage and fresh elections, and simultaneously sent the CRS to break up key industrial occupations, and by the end of June the university buildings were regained. Lyndon Johnson's successor Richard Nixon continued the war in Vietnam for five more years, and detonated more explosive power on non-combatants Cambodia and Laos than had been used in all previous human conflict combined. Democratic reforms in Northern Ireland sparked anti-Catholic pogroms by the Protestant majority and in 1972 the British Army created the conditions for 25 years of anti-imperialist war in Ireland by killing 14 unarmed civil rights protesters on Bloody Sunday and invading Free Derry. Student movements were central to all these developments, and their failure greatly influenced a generation of scholarship about the production and consumption of artistic works within capitalist society.

In the disillusionment of the late 1960s, poststructuralism/deconstruction was attractive. The fault, it seemed to many, lay in certainties and grand generalizations, and deconstruction sought always to undermine dichotomies, to reject binaries (including left/right in politics), and to embrace pluralities and undecidabilities. In place of grand narratives and projects, political radicalism sought local engagements such as communes, refuges for battered women, and self-help groups. In literary studies, poststructuralism/deconstruction suggested the futility of attempting to relate the work to history, since historiography itself was corrupted by the taint of language, an ideological construct. Rather than seeing things how they were, historiography might simply be writing its own internal structures onto the past, not 'history' but, in a pun that appealed to feminists, 'his story'.

If all constructs could be made to dismantle themselves, there was little point attempting to account for something as palpably self-deluding as, say, 'the critical developments of the eighteenth century', but one might still return to the internal structure of a sonnet to demonstrate that it is created from false distinctions. Giving voice to the foul-mouthed unconscious of the most civilized discourse and reading against the grain to show what must be suppressed for coherent meaning to emerge were ways to continue radical activity inside academia. Deconstruction as practised by the Yale school of Connecticut was little different from the formalism of New Criticism, but done in the name of revealing the secret deceptions at the heart of previous scholarship. Deconstruction shared Marxism's scepticism of inherited conceptual categories and its relish for self-contradiction, but drew from them a grim conviction that progress itself is merely an illusion created by naive optimism. This gloom fed into postmodernism, aptly summarized by Jean-François Lyotard as 'incredulity towards metanarratives' (Lyotard 1984, xxiv), where 'metanarratives' are seen as explanations that invoke ultimate, fundamental processes.

Nineteen sixty-eight was a turning point in the theorizing of the relationship between politics and culture, but the only raised consciousness that can truly be said to have immediately produced new critical theory was feminism. In the 1970s critics explored new subject positions from which to perceive the past, and working-class history, women's history, and the history of oppressed races became legitimate studies, but in Shakespeare studies, feminism alone stood as an example of radical politics feeding cultural theory and critical practice. This changed, however, with the publication of Stephen Greenblatt's *Renaissance Self-Fashioning* (1980), which launched a new critical paradigm from the platform of ideas first proposed by the Marxist Raymond Williams.

Raymond Williams to Stephen Greenblatt: The New Historicism

Williams had not abandoned metanarratives; instead he nuanced Marxist cultural theory. For his model of 'Dominant, Residual, and Emergent' cultures (Williams 1977, 121–7) Williams borrowed from dialectical materialism the idea that although history can be divided into epochs (feudal, capitalist, communist), at any moment there are new ways of thinking and doing being born, others reaching their zenith, and others that are dying (Stalin 1941, 6–9). The phases of birth, growth, and death are no more separated in history than in an individual's life. The important thing for practical politics is to distinguish which trends will grow and might usefully be pursued and which should be abandoned as in decay.

Aspects of a culture entirely consigned to the past Williams called 'archaic' to distinguish them from the 'residual' ones that, although originating in the past, have an active function in the present:

Thus organized religion is predominantly residual, but within this there is a significant difference between some practically alternative and oppositional meanings and values (absolute brotherhood, service to others without reward) and a larger body of incorporated meanings and values (official morality, or the social order of which the other-worldly is a separated neutralizing or ratifying component). (Williams 1977, 122)

Residual culture can still be oppositional, as when priests condemn government policy, although it might also have archaisms in it.

Emergent culture is the hardest to identify since the future is necessarily murkier than the past and anything that we hope will be progressive can always be subverted by incorporation into the dominant culture. The prototypical case is the emergence of working-class culture in nineteenth-century England:

A new class is always a source of emergent cultural practice, but while it is still, as a class, relatively subordinate, this is always likely to be uneven and is certain to be incomplete. . . . Straight incorporation is most directly attempted against the visibly alternative and oppositional class elements: trade unions, working-class political parties, working-class life styles (as incorporated into 'popular' journalism, advertising, and commercial entertainment). (Williams 1977, 124)

Dominant culture, then, is a partial affair: '. . . no mode of production and therefore no dominant social order and therefore no dominant culture ever in reality includes or exhausts all human practice, human energy, and human intention', and not because modes of domination overlook the residual and the emergent but because '. . . they select from and consequently exclude the full range of human practice' (Williams 1977, 125).

The Marxist concept of reification, the turning of active labour into solid objects, lies behind Williams's puzzling oxymoron 'structures of feeling'. We tend to discuss culture and society in the past tense, to convert social experience into finished products:

The point is especially relevant to works of art, which really are, in one sense, explicit and finished forms—actual objects in the visual arts, objectified conventions and notations (semantic figures) in literature. But it is not only that, to complete their inherent process, we have to make them present, in specifically active 'readings'. It is also that the making of art is never itself in the past tense. It is always a formative process, within a specific present. (Williams 1977, 129)

At the start of the twenty-first century there is universal agreement that Shakespeare's works are necessarily incomplete, finished only in the acts of performance and in criticism—even the British national curriculum for school teaching promotes this view—and it is easy to under-appreciate how unusual Williams's claim was 25 years ago, when various kinds of formalism dominated literary studies.

Slipping into the past tense and into fixed forms is necessary for historical study, but we should always remain aware of its reductiveness:

Perhaps the dead can be reduced to fixed forms, though their surviving records are against it. But the living will not be reduced, at least in the first person; living third persons may be different. All the known complexities, the experienced tensions, shifts, and uncertainties, the intricate forms of unevenness and confusion, are against the terms of the reduction and soon, by extension, against social analysis itself. (Williams 1977, 129–30)

The fixed forms (mental categories) with which we explain the world to ourselves are never quite up to the job: 'There is frequent tension between the received interpretation and practical experience' and this creates new, inchoate interpretative categories that Williams called 'structures of feeling', or 'structures of experience', although the latter does not imply pastness (Williams 1977, 130–2).

A 'structure of feeling' is something of a cultural hypothesis, not yet confirmed and turned into a fixed form, and

The hypothesis has a special relevance to art and literature, where the true social content is in a significant number of cases of this present and affective kind, which cannot without loss be reduced to belief systems, institutions, or explicit general relationships, though it may include all these as lived and experienced, with or without tension, as it also evidently includes elements of social and material (physical or natural) experience which may lie beyond, or be uncovered or imperfectly covered by, the elsewhere recognizable systematic elements. (Williams 1977, 133)

Lest this might simply be thought another way of saying that one cannot pin down art, Williams gave a concrete example in relation to early Victorian ideology, which 'specified the exposure caused by poverty or by debt or by illegitimacy as social failure or deviation', while in the work of Charles Dickens and Emily Brontë we see a 'structure of feeling' that showed 'exposure and isolation as a *general* condition, and poverty, debt, or illegitimacy as its connecting instances' (Williams 1977, 134).

As a Fulbright scholar in Cambridge in the mid-1960s, Stephen Greenblatt found in the lectures of Raymond Williams 'all that had been carefully excluded from the literary criticism in which I had been trained—who controlled access to the printing press, who owned the land and the factories, whose voices were being repressed as well as represented in literary texts, what social strategies were being served by the aesthetic values we constructed' and all these 'came pressing back in upon the act of interpretation' (Greenblatt 1990, 2). The complex interrelation of consciousness and external social forms that Williams meant by a 'structure of feeling' is what Greenblatt explored in *Renaissance Self-Fashioning*, which began

...there is in the early modern period a change in the intellectual, social, psychological, and aesthetic structures that govern the generation of identities. This change is difficult to characterize in our usual ways because it is not only complex but resolutely dialectical. (Greenblatt 1980, 1)

For Greenblatt, consciousness necessarily arose from social being:

...in Italy in the later Middle Ages, the transition from feudalism to despotism, fostered a radical change in consciousness: the princes and *condottieri*, and their secretaries, ministers, poets, and followers, were cut off from established forms of identity.... (Greenblatt 1980, 161–2)

They found a new means to fashion their own identities using rhetoric and its related armoury of intellectual skills including theatricality and manners.

Greenblatt reported that when he began the book he was convinced of the individual's ability to fashion his own identity:

But as my work progressed, I perceived that fashioning oneself and being fashioned by cultural institutions—family, religion, stage—were inseparably intertwined. In all my texts and documents, there were, so far as I could tell, no moments of pure, unfettered subjectivity; indeed, the human subject itself began to seem remarkably unfree, the ideological product of the relations of power in a particular society. (Greenblatt 1980, 256)

One need not change one's view that consciousness arises from social being (the Marxist insight) to move from optimism to pessimism about human intellectual freedom, but only if one is ultimately more optimistic than pessimistic can one really be a Marxist.

'The Circulation of Social Energy' is Greenblatt's clearest statement of his methodology, what he wanted to call a 'poetics of culture' but which became known as the New Historicism. Greenblatt took from Williams his rejection of the Formalist and New Critical notion of 'the "text itself" as the perfect, unsubstitutable, freestanding container of all of its meanings' because '... there is no escape from contingency' (Greenblatt 1988, 3), and he was concerned to take seriously 'the collective production of literary pleasure and interest', which derives from language itself, 'the supreme instance of collective creation' (Greenblatt 1988, 4).

Greenblatt thought the Renaissance theatre to be inherently collectivist, in its modes of creation (the use of sources and habits of collaboration) and its mode of performance that 'depends upon a felt community: there is no dimming of lights, no attempt to isolate and awaken the sensibilities of each individual member of the audience, no sense of the disappearance of the crowd' (Greenblatt 1988, 5). The power of cultural artefacts (especially the plays of Shakespeare) to continue to 'arouse disquiet, pain, fear, the beating of the heart, pity, laughter, tension, relief, wonder' Greenblatt attributed to the 'social energy' encoded within them (Greenblatt 1988, 6), whereas most 'collective expressions moved from their original setting to a new place or time are dead on arrival' (Greenblatt 1988, 7).

Progressive as it was, Greenblatt's New Historicism helped to popularize a view that has done much harm to radical politics: anti-essentialism. Greenblatt repeated Clifford Geertz's assertion that 'There is no such thing as a human nature independent of culture ... ' (Greenblatt 1980, 3), which should alert us to how he came to his pessimistic conclusion that there is no such thing as unfettered subjectivity. To see why, we must digress to clarify philosophical terminology that has been misused in recent work on Shakespeare.

Anti-essentialism and Anti-idealism

One might defend Geertz's statement as meaning that humans cannot exist alone—after all without adult attention an infant quickly dies—so that 'culture' (most broadly defined as the actions of others) intervenes from the day one is born. However, that is clearly not what Geertz meant by culture, and rather he was making the relativist (that is, anti-essentialist) claim that things we might take for granted as unchangeable aspects of being human (emotions, for example) are in fact historically and culturally contingent. This might seem like a Marxist 'step back' to turn a given into a construct, but it is primarily a linguistic gesture, expanding the second term in the binary opposition nature/culture to encompass everything so that there is nothing left for it to distinguish itself from. The same inflation, but in the opposite direction, occurs in Polixenes's claim that 'nature is made better by no mean / But nature makes that mean' (*The Winter's Tale* 4.4.89–90), swallowing up all human horticultural intervention that Perdita calls 'art'.

Were Geertz right, even my laughter when watching Oliver Hardy's eyes widen at another of Stan Laurel's mistakes would not be an expression of my human nature, only of a particular culture against which one might compare another in which this non-verbal signal has a different meaning, or is meaningless. Fortunately, Geertz is wrong and recent anthropological work has shown that the facial expressions associated with various emotions are truly transcultural, and this point will be picked up in the conclusion. It is enough to note here that such extreme relativism, evident also in the claim that 'everything is political', is politically debilitating since it leaves us nothing (not even the pleasure of a belly laugh) in which we might invest significant human value; if even hunger is merely a cultural construct rather than an absolute there seems little reason to object to it.

Marx was not anti-essentialist and described as 'species-being' or 'species-nature' the human creative productivity of all kinds that is noticeably lacking in other animals and exists apart from politics and culture (Marx 1977, 67–9). Without such a model of human nature specific political and cultural struggles have no object worth the fight.

Just as Saussure's structuralist linguistics retains its power only in literary studies, the linguists long ago having adopted Chomsky's transformational-generative grammar, so cultural relativity reigns in literary studies despite the overwhelming evidence that innate traits— including the capacity for language, in Chomsky's view—really exist.

Materialists follow Marx in concerning themselves with the hard facts about the world (including economics) rather than the soft ideas, and as Catherine Belsey put it, they reject 'the idealist tendency to analyse love and ignore money' (Belsey 1991, 258). The rejection of idealism might come as a surprise to those unused to philosophical theory: surely Marxism is inherently idealistic? In imagining an ideal form of human society in which no one has to work more hours than are necessary to produce the value that she wishes to consume, it is idealistic. However, in a precise philosophical sense it is not, since it asserts the primacy of material reality over ideas.

There are several strands of idealism in philosophy, including subjective idealism, transcendental idealism, and absolute idealism, but they can roughly be divided into two classes. The first is metaphysical idealism, which asserts that reality is just an effect of ideas, whether those are being thought by the Universal Mind (as Hegel had it) or by God (as the theistic idealists believe). The opposite of metaphysical idealism is materialism, which insists that the basic stuff of the universe is matter and that we know about it through its material form. The second kind of idealism is epistemological idealism, which insists that regardless of how the world actually *is* we can know about it only through our minds, so what we share when we discuss it are reports of the psychical processes in our heads. The opposite of this insistence that our minds mediate reality (and so perception fundamentally conditions our sense of what reality is) is realism, which insists that human knowledge grasps things as they really are in the world.

These distinctions are often blurred in literary studies, most damagingly when materialism, the metaphysical opposite to idealism, is treated as its epistemological opposite too, although this is properly realism. The reason radical criticism has insisted on epistemological idealism seems to be the desire to assert, as the title of Peter L. Berger and Thomas Luckman's book has it, *The Social Construction of Reality* (1967). The patent silliness of this claim has been no barrier to its widescale acceptance in academic circles while the rest of the world continues with realism, as when Jean Baudrillard used his theory of simulations to argue in the French newspaper *Libération* on 4 January 1991 (two weeks before Operation Desert Storm) that the Gulf War could not happen, and then on 29 March (a month after the American ceasefire) that indeed it had not occurred. While clearly intended as a provocative gesture and not a statement of truth, Baudrillard's book *The Gulf War Did Not Take Place* (1995) is typical of postmodernism's irritatingly airy dismissal of realism.

In *Radical Tragedy* (1984) Jonathan Dollimore took up this matter in a final section called 'Subjectivity: Idealism versus Materialism' (Dollimore 1984, 247–71). Dollimore declared the target of his anti-humanism: 'the idea that "man" possesses some given, unalterable essence which is what makes "him" human, which is the source and *essential* determinant of "his" culture and its priority over conditions of existence' (Dollimore 1984, 250). A belief in human essence is part of many religions, but it is also a part of Marxism, via 'species-being'. Indeed, without such a notion it is hard to imagine why anyone would consider the project of freeing human beings to have priority over other concerns.

Further, it is self-evident that being human is an essential determinant of our culture, for possession of opposable thumbs and finely controllable larynxes containing vocal chords, together with brains much bigger than we need for the basic tasks of survival, is undeniably part of the reason we write, speak, and theorize about the past. That this culture has 'priority over conditions of existence' is more problematic: a Marxist would not want to assert that culture is detached from 'conditions of existence', but nor would she want to insist that it is entirely controlled by conditions of existence either, and indeed much of the present book has been concerned with precisely what is the relationship between conditions of existence and culture.

Dollimore wanted to unseat (or, in his terminology, decentre) the notion of human nature because it had been used to explain as inevitable events that he thought were explicable by historical circumstance. He argued that rather than validating the conservative idea that a tragic hero falls because of some flaw in himself, Renaissance tragedy tends to show the contingent causes of the situations depicted. A fixed human nature, then, leads to a fixed human history, for we are all doomed to badness before we start: 'When existing political conditions are thus thought to be as unalterable as the fixed human condition of which they are, allegedly, only a reflection, then salvation comes, typically to be located in the pseudo-religious absolute of Personal Integrity' (Dollimore 1984, 268).

In fact the fixity of politics does not necessarily follow from the alleged fixity of human nature, and indeed those involved in the most protracted political struggles often report that the greatest joy is in collective overcoming of deeply ingrained human foibles. Without amenities, the most determined Greenham Common peace campaigner could, it is true, be tempted away to the comforts of bath, bed, and breakfast, and, true, factional in-fighting did lead to the formation of two opposed camps outside neighbouring gates, an ironic mirror of the international situation that the Greenham base's Cruise missiles were supposed to regulate. However, anyone who has lived with the politically committed can testify that they tend to rise early in the morning (to steal a march on their opponents), to think more creatively about the means of their resistance than their opponents do about the oppression, and generally to suppress their meaner natures for the sake of collective progress. It is hardly conservative to claim that human beings tend to fall short of their ideals, and indeed one might argue that this shortfall is human nature and an important engine of progress. We may marvel at what can be achieved *despite* human nature and there is no prior obligation to deny human nature in order to encompass political progress.

Much feminism of the late 1960s and early 1970s was unashamedly essentialist: men were the problem that women had to find solutions to, or in the more radical view move away from. While there might be debate about just how men and women were, there was little debate about whether it was appropriate to discuss the matter in such essentialist terms, about whether it made sense to speak of how men 'are'. However, Simone de Beauvoir had claimed that 'One is not born, but rather becomes, a woman' (De Beauvoir 1953, 273), invoking a distinction between femaleness (the innate characteristics derived from possession of XX chromosomes) and femininity (the social concomitants of being perceived to be female). As we have seen, in 1982 Linda Bamber took it as understood that 'Men must write as men and women as women . . . ' (Bamber 1982, 5), but through the 1980s materialism came to be understood as more or less the same thing as the rejection of such essentialism.

A typical example that flits between metaphysical materialism and epistemological idealism is Valerie Wayne's introduction to the volume of essays *The Matter of Difference: Materialist Feminist Criticism of Shakespeare* (1991):

> While materialist feminism is not simply criticism about the physical matter associated with women's bodies, for instance, it can apply to our bodies as sites for the inscriptions of ideology and power, since we cannot 'know' them in any unmediated form and they, as we, are products of the cultural meanings ascribed to them. Althusser's theory [of ideology] enables critical connections between the various meanings of the word [material] and impedes any simple opposition between mind or consciousness and body. (Wayne 1991, 8)

Wayne is quite right about the central issue for a discussion of ideology—mediation between consciousness and the body—but rather overstates the success of Althusser's theory, which, as we saw in Chapter 1, attributes so much to the social construction (by 'interpellation') of the individual's sense of herself that it is a wonder anyone can think for themselves at all. As Lukács showed (pp. 31–2, 56–8 above), what is needed here is Marx's insight that self-knowledge is the category that mediates between consciousness and body, locking them into a progressive dialectic.

Cultural Materialism

Where Marx most clearly influences present Shakespeare studies is in Cultural Materialism, a term imported from anthropology and first used in relation to literature by Raymond Williams, for whom it was 'a theory of the specificities of material cultural and literary production within historical materialism' (Williams 1977, 5). The landmark publication was *Political Shakespeare: New Essays in Cultural Materialism* (1985), edited by Jonathan Dollimore and Alan Sinfield. Put crudely, Cultural Materialism is the British version of New Historicism with which it shares a concern for marginal histories and for finding the politics embedded in literary works, but where the American variant quickly marked itself off from feminism, British Cultural Materialism embraced it.

In an afterword to Dollimore and Sinfield's book, Williams wrote about two critical responses to historical context. One is to deny its importance so that Shakespeare and his modern readers are linked 'through experience of a radically continuous human nature' and we understand Hamlet's problems 'by the more rather than the less [we have] in common'. The other response is to overstate the importance of history, to assert that the very words being read, as well as the beliefs about them and the actions undertaken in their name, have changed so much since Shakespeare's time that we risk total miscomprehension unless (and possibly even if) we immerse ourselves in what is recoverable of the past (Williams 1985, 234). The New Historicism tends to the latter and Cultural Materialism quite rightly leans on the former simply because it is more politically engaged. After all, if life in Shakespeare's time was utterly unlike life now there would be little reason to bother with the past in the effort to shape the future. If, however, the past greatly differed from the present, but in intelligible ways, this at least proves that a thorough transformation of society is possible: if it happened before, it can happen again.

An oddly liberal American, and un-Marxist, note was sounded by Dollimore and Sinfield's introduction to the volume, which distanced their concerns from those of 'much established literary criticism' that tries to mystify its perspective as 'the natural, obvious or right interpretation' of the text—not, one hopes, to be replaced by transparent, wrong interpretations—and they made the curious claim that the new approach 'On the contrary... registers its commitment to the transformation of a social order which exploits people on grounds of race, gender, and class' (Dollimore and Sinfield 1985a, viii). It is difficult to see how this is 'contrary' to its antecedent, but more worrying still is the idea that capitalist society exploits on the grounds of class, here likened to the categories of race and gender. One can see where a social-constructionist view of history might lead: race, gender, and class are categories (defined by material difference) created by the prevailing social order, which then exploits people for belonging to the wrong one(s).

Where Marx would of course disagree is about the category class, which he thought merely a convenient generalization about people's relations to production, and the most important category simply because capitalism will necessarily cast greater numbers of people into one class, the proletariat, until that class is large enough to overthrow the bourgeoisie. Nobody wants to be poor, of course, but it is far from clear that everyone wants to be released from the categories of race and gender; if only being a woman did not entail doing more housework and earning less money than men, it would not of itself seem a condition of oppression. Likewise, those in Britain's first overseas colony have long struggled to be free, but have tended to consider their oppression in terms of the economic wealth extracted from their island rather than in the condition of simply being Irish. By likening race, gender, and class, Dollimore and Sinfield abandoned the Marxist insight that class is a unique category, not an incidental attribute by which one might be oppressed, and without this the political project diminishes to liberal reformism that treats the social order as a given and hopes only for a meritocracy in which being from the wrong race, gender, or class would be no barrier to advancement.

Also published in 1985 was a collection of essays, *Alternative Shakespeares* edited by John Drakakis, whose title was intended to signal the rejection of a single, stable subject for Shakespeare studies and the insistence that acts of criticism created their own subject as they proceed. This was the point that we saw Marxist Alick West explicitly denying in the previous chapter (p. 60 above) and one that Terence Hawkes made the subject of his influential book, *Meaning by Shakespeare* (1992). A grave weakness of New Historicism and Cultural Materialism has been a misplaced confidence that Althusser's theorizing of ideology solved the problems of determination, consciousness, and base/superstructure that we have been considering. A typical essay from Drakakis's collection illustrates how badly this misplaced confidence can affect Shakespeare criticism.

James H. Kavanagh's essay offered the over-simplified summation of Althusser's view that ideology is 'a system of representations that offer the subject an imaginary, compelling, sense of reality in which crucial contradictions of self and social order appear resolved' (Kavanagh 1985, 145). Kavanagh wished to attend to the historical conditions under which Shakespeare worked, as any Marxist critic should, and characterized them as 'semi-independence between patronage and the market, while still under severe ideological compulsion—dependent on the whims of court and council, caught in the ideological space between modified absolutism and insurgent Puritanism' (Kavanagh 1985, 149–50). What has been seen as the Elizabethan golden age was really just a 'temporary and precarious stabilization of conflicting social projects' (Kavanagh 1985, 150) that merely deferred the inevitable revolution.

This account lacked a sense that although the new joint-stock companies (including the playing troupes) were proto-capitalist and operated outside the regulatory systems of the guild structure they depended on monopolies granted by the monarch. As Belsey observed, the selling of monopolies was one of the means by which the Tudors and Stuarts sought to evade parliamentary control (Belsey 1985b, 93), so that rather than a simple struggle between the old feudal ways embodied in a modified monarchy and the demands of the rising urban bourgeoisie, the situation was truly dialectical: the aristocracy, not the bourgeoisie, created the conditions for wealth accumulation that made Britain the first capitalist economy.

Together, these errors led Kavanagh to perceive the allegedly proto-bourgeois artisans (carpenter, weaver, bellows-mender, tinker, and tailor) of *A Midsummer Night's Dream* as essentially like a real playing company, treading the precarious path of pleasurably transporting their aristocratic audience (to win approval) without 'disrupt[ing] *their* lived relation to the real, [which] would be an unacceptable usurpation of ideological power' (Kavanagh 1985, 153–4). Like Brecht, Kavanagh wanted to valourize the 'workers' troupe' (they switch from proto-bourgeoisie to proto-proletariat as Kavanagh's argument demands), so he imagined them as Shakespeare's comedic version of his own company, created to trivialize the all-too-real threat under which he and his fellows worked. Ideology is the work of resolving the latest contradictions that the social organization of labour throws up, and in this play, Kavanagh claimed, the resolution is achieved by shared comic closure.

This reading leaves unexplained the intense derision that most producers of the play find in its final scene. In truth, the play's mechanicals are nothing like Shakespeare's company, and it was precisely because there existed professional acting troupes (who were not simply taking a break from their daytime labour), and because they were sponsored by the aristocracy, that the amateurs of Athens can safely be laughed at. If they stood for anything in the economic organization of Elizabethan London it was the long-standing guild structure, not the new joint-stock playing companies.

For explanatory purposes one might crudely summarize Althusser's performative model of ideology as 'you are what you do', inasmuch as he thought of the relationship between social forces and the individual as a kind of dramatic casting of role that makes one feel individually appreciated (by personal 'hailing') when in truth any person could take one's place. It is easy to overstate the importance that living a role has, and no one should understand De Beauvoir's claim that 'One is not born, but rather becomes, a woman' as a denial of biological reality. However, extraordinarily, an apparently Marxist approach can lead to the claim that in the Renaissance people really did worry that men would turn into women if they acted like them. An often-cited argument for this repays close inspection for it illustrates how far anti-essentialism (believed by its adherents to be a Marxist principle) can distort an historical-literary reading.

Laura Levine found a contradiction in the Renaissance anti-theatricalists' claim that men dressing as women is an abominable rebellion against the divine order that inheres in sex-difference. Were sex identity really divinely ordered, Levine reasoned, cross-dressing would be harmless for one would remain *really* male or female underneath; the protestations actually speak of a fear that clothes, and gender performance in general, make us who we are. In fact, in the tracts 'The assumption is that "doing" is constitutive' (Levine 1986, 125). However, the anti-theatricalists also wrote that theatre releases the latent beastliness of humankind, and here Levine saw a contradiction: 'They subscribe simultaneously to a view of the self as pliable, manipulable, easily unshaped, and at the same time to a view of the self as monstrous' (Levine 1986, 127–8). That is, the self is 'really nothing at all' and at the same time 'already an insatiable monster' (Levine 1986, 128).

This logical inconsistency, Levine decided, the anti-theatricalists resolved in 'banish[ing] the notion of the self as monster' by projecting it onto actors, and hence their vitriol about the stage. However, that projection still left the anti-theatricalists holding onto a relativistic sense of self—in which 'doing' is constitutive of 'being'—and Levine found an increasingly frantic attempt to assert an essentialist model of selfhood while making attacks whose logic is relativistic.

Levine was mistaken: the claimed relativism does not exist in the documents she cited, for as she admitted '. . . [Stephen] Gosson never explicitly claims that signs are constitutive' and the one moment when

Philip Stubbes seems unequivocal on the matter he is in fact para-phrasing Gosson:

Our apparel was given us as a sign distinctive, to discern betwixt sex and sex, and therefore one to wear the apparel of another sex is to participate with the same, and to adulterate the verity of his own kind. (Stubbes 2002, 118)

Levine quoted the last clause as 'the merits of his own kinde' (Levine 1986, 134), a reading not found in any early printing according to Margaret Jane Kidnie's collation, and she corrected this in the book-length version of the argument (Levine 1994, 22).

To adulterate, however, is not to change the nature of something entirely but rather to corrupt it by adding inferior stuff, and as Kidnie noted (Stubbes 2002, 32) Levine's argument was greatly weakened by the passage in question being about female, not male, cross-dressers. In both versions of the essay Levine claimed that 'Men and women who wear each other's costume, says Stubbes, "may not improperly be called Hermaphrodites, that is, Monsters of both kindes, half women, half men"' (Levine 1986, 134), but a glance at Stubbes shows that he was writing only about women, so it is not a claim of effeminization at all. The rest of Levine's evidence pointed the other way, indicating an essentialist confidence that 'doing' cannot alter one's 'being'.

Most importantly, Levine ignored Christian theology's subtlety in these matters. Her perceived tension between 'a view of the self as pliable, manipulable, easily unshaped' and 'a view of the self as monstrous' is already encompassed in the doctrines of free will and original sin. Even Luther and Calvin, who disagreed with Erasmus about the philosophical validity of using the label 'freedom' for acts that are predestined, accepted that certain acts (sins) run counter to God's general guidelines for human behaviour and that Christian faith requires patient acceptance of the ticklish paradox of an all-loving God having a divine plan that includes the local triumphs of evil.

Condemnations of cross-dressing discouraged sin and so were predicated on the freedom to choose Christian obedience. Were it thought that 'doing' might transmute into 'being' there would be little reason to worry since the disjunction between clothing and sex would disappear. Clothes can only be deemed inappropriate for an individual's sex if the self is indeed unalterable, so these tracts actually speak of the durability of essentialism, not its collapse.

John Lyly's play *Galatea* (first performed 1584–8) dramatized the essentialist view. Two girls are dressed as boys by their parents and each falls in love with the other thinking her a boy. There is homoerotic frisson in their uncertainty—each suspects the truth about the other— but since they are heterosexual one of them must become actually male for pleasure to be attained, and this only Venus can effect. This ending is undoubtedly heterocentric, but importantly it is essentialist: dress- ing-up did not change assigned identity.

In a new introduction for the second edition of *Radical Tragedy* (1989), Dollimore linked Levine's argument to Michel Foucault's claim that homosexuality too was about 'doing' not 'being' and did not become an identity until the nineteenth century: 'Before that individuals were regarded as performing deviant sexual *acts*, but an intrinsic *identity* was not attributed to, or assumed by, them...' (Dollimore 1989, xxxvii). Thus, claimed Alan Bray, 'To talk of an individual in this period as being or not being "a homosexual" is an anachronism...' (Bray 1982, 16). Joseph Cady has shown that Foucault's and Bray's claims are simply contradicted by the currency of the expression 'masculine love' appearing in Francis Bacon's *New Atlantis* (1627) and Thomas Heywood's *Pleasant Dialogues and Dramas* (1637) (Cady 1992).

The materialism of Cultural Materialism is supposed to ground the criticism in what actually happened in Shakespeare's time and to avoid imposing modern concepts and categories on its allegedly alien cul- ture. Just as our thinking about dress and sexuality might be radically different from theirs, so, it is claimed, are our ways of understanding theatrical performance. As we have seen, Brecht thought Shakespeare's was a theatre 'full of A[lienation]-effects' (Brecht 1965, 58), if only we can rediscover them. New Historicists and Cultural Materialists have often claimed that spectators at a dramatic performance tended to hold the performer and the role quite separate, whereas we tend to collapse this 'double vision' into a singularity.

Unfortunately, what little evidence we have points the other way: the first audiences, like us, tended to get swept away by emotional identification with the plays' characters, as Richard Levin showed (Levin 1980, 11–21). In Thomas Nashe's account of the death of Talbot in 1 *Henry VI*, the actors brought forth 'the tears of ten thousand spectators at least, (at several times) who, in the tragedian that represents his person, imagine they behold him fresh bleeding!' (Salgādo 1975, 16). In Henry Jackson's eyewitness account of a performance of *Othello* at Oxford in 1610 the actor playing Desdemona is described as if female: 'she always acted her whole part supremely well, yet when she was killed she was even more moving, for when she fell back upon the bed she implored the pity of the spectators by her very face' (Salgādo 1975, 30).

Richard Burbage was repeatedly praised for seeming to become the role he played, and an anonymous funeral elegy describes how as 'young Hamlet.../ kind Lear, the grieved Moor, and more beside' Burbage's naturalism reached such a perfection and was 'So lively, that spectators, and the rest / Of his sad crew, whilst he but seemed to bleed, / Amazed, thought even then he died indeed' (Salgādo 1975, 38–9). Richard Flecknoe made the same claim about Burbage 'so wholly transforming himself into his part, and putting off himself with his clothes, as he never (not so much as in the tyring-house) assumed himself again until the play was done' (Chambers 1923, 370). Regarding a good actor performing 'any bold English man' in any English history play, Thomas Heywood insisted that in his patriotism an audience member was necessarily swept away by emotional identification, 'pursuing him [the actor] in his [the role's] enterprise with his [the spectator's] best wishes, and, as being wrapped in contemplation, offers to him in his heart all prosperous performance, as if the personater were the man personated, so bewitching a thing is lively and well spirited action' (Chambers 1923, 251).

Brecht's claim, and more recent versions of it, cannot then stand as absolute: sometimes Shakespeare's first audiences *were* carried away by the emotions generated by an actor immersed in his role. But how much of the time, and why then? In a section on 'Role and Actor' in his *Shakespeare and the Popular Tradition in the Theater* (in German, 1967), and in an article (Weimann 1988), the German Marxist Robert Weimann related this matter to the spatial arrangements on the stage during performance.

An actor going near to the edge of the stage (*platea*) in an open-air amphitheatre, near to the audience, somewhat came out of his role and from this dislocated position he could comment upon it, while near the back wall (where important characters mostly stood) official doctrines were promulgated and accepted:

Logically, in light of stage action and social convention, the speaker from the throne was raised physically above those around him and did not function on a level of direct audience contact.... In terms of theatrical history this mode of presentation corresponded to the use of the scaffold as *locus* where... the ruling and high-born characters sat.... But downstage, somewhere in between the socially and spatially elevated Claudius and Timon and the audience, stood characters less inclined to accept the assumptions—social, ideological, and dramatic—of the localized action. These characters, by means of aside, wordplay, proverbs, and direct audience address offered a special perspective to the audience. (Weimann 1978, 221–2)

Although an upstage/downstage distinction is not quite right for the level thrust stages of Shakespeare's time, Weimann's scale of degree to which an actor might, at any one time, be immersed in his role is more sophisticated than the bald claims that he never was. A Marxist approach to Shakespeare does not need the vulgarities of crude over-statement, nor must it—as historians often accuse Cultural Material-ism and New Historicism—ignore historical evidence.

Subversion/Containment and Teleological Thinking

Shakespeare is the most widely taught writer in capitalist societies, and the claim often made by Marxist-inspired critics that his works are subversive allows them to reconcile their political and professional impulses: they can continue teaching Shakespeare but in a way that celebrates not his capturing of human nature but his interrogation of the major political and philosophical ideas of his age. The danger is that if they are wrong—if his works are conservative—then the radical scholars are actually serving capitalism's 'containment' of subversion. In an essay that tackled this matter directly, Kathleen McLuskie saw a way out of the simple dichotomy—Is Shakespeare conservative or radical?—in 'refusing to construct an author behind the plays' and instead attending to the 'textual strategies [that] limit the range of meaning which the text allows' (McLuskie 1985, 92).

Others have gone further and argued that there is no such thing as the 'meaning' (*noun*) of Shakespeare at all, for meanings are provi-sional and constructed afresh by each age's interpretation of him. In Terence Hawkes's title *Meaning by Shakespeare*, meaning is a verb: the way that we do our meaning via our readings of Shakespeare. This attractive idea has a logical limit, of course, since if there is no possibility of returning to the original meanings (*noun*) of past works then Hawkes's book of more than a decade ago has itself slipped beyond our grasp, and by extension even the one you are holding can be experienced only as an artefact of its time, no matter when you are reading this; indeed it is not one artefact at all, being composed of chapters written in historical contexts separated by three years (2001–3). This extremist view drains the rhetorical force from even an urgent exhortation, and in practice the most relativistic of deconstructionists overcome their qualms when it suits them. In theory one might accept that an utterance's original meaning is irrecoverable a split second after it falls from a speaker's lips, but one still leaves a crowded building upon hearing the cry 'Fire!'

New Historicism has tended to see containment outdoing subversion, and Greenblatt's much-reprinted essay 'Invisible Bullets' argued that the theatre industry of Shakespeare's time was a special device for the containment of progressive forces precisely because it appeared to produce subversion. Greenblatt first showed this phenomenon operating in another context: Thomas Harriot's report of Algonkian Indians coming to doubt their own religion and taking up the Christianity of their colonizers. According to Greenblatt, Harriot's account shows that in imposing his religion upon the natives, Harriot exposed the truth of 'the most radically subversive hypothesis in his culture', namely that religion is just a way of keeping fools in awe in order more efficiently to exploit them (Greenblatt 1985, 23). Thus subversive ideas might be in the service of their own containment, since Harriot's ends were not liberative but colonial and to subdue the natives he might test and confirm any heresy. Although it does not affect my argument, Greenblatt's was an entirely unfounded attack on Harriot's reputation, for he was no colonial lackey (Sokol 1994).

Greenblatt found the same principle in 'Shakespeare's drama, written for a theatre subject to State censorship' that was allowed to be subversive because finally Renaissance power 'contains the radical doubts it continually provokes' (Greenblatt 1985, 45). In an ambiguous pair of closing sentences Greenblatt wrote that '...we are free to locate and pay homage to the plays' doubts only because they no longer threaten us. There is subversion, no end of subversion, only not for us' (Greenblatt 1985, 45). This might suggest a pattern of repetition: just as prince Hal indulges Falstaff and his tavern companions (in 1 *Henry IV*) in order to better understand and eventually contain such subversive forces (in 2 *Henry IV*), so we critics fantasize that our commentaries are subversive but capitalism's superstructure (especially universities and theatres) ultimately contain them.

Containment might follow hard on any subversion, as suggested by Belsey's comment that no matter how much freedom a Portia, Viola, or Rosalind might achieve in the middle of a play, 'At the end of each story the heroine abandons her disguise and dwindles into a wife' (Belsey 1985a, 187). In a way the difference between Cultural Materialists and New Historicists might, then, be simply a difference between an optimistic privileging of Acts 2, 3, and 4 on the part of the former and a pessimistic privileging of Act 5 by the latter. In Greenblatt's case, the pessimistic note is sounded at the end of each critical work, a feature of *Renaissance Self-Fashioning* and 'Invisible Bullets', as though a necessary counterpart to his own cessation.

From this perspective, the New Historicists are, perhaps surprisingly, showing a teleological sensibility: their enjoyment of the liberations of Acts 2–4 is always tainted by the knowledge of the coming containment; they could use a Brechtian reminder that this need not be the case. That is to say, dramatic outcomes follow a script but history does not. In the case of Shakespeare, however, the script itself often deviates from conventional expectation, lurching from comedy to tragedy with the death of Mercutio in *Romeo and Juliet* or, even more strikingly, in the final disasters of *King Lear* that must have come as a surprise to anyone who thought they knew the story since the sources all end more happily.

Especially interesting in this regard is a play's apparent refusal to end at all or the projection of its own ending beyond the formal closure of audience applause. Viola is to retain her disguise as Cesario until after her 'other habits' are found, which means catching up with Malvolio and finding from him the whereabouts of the sea captain that has them. Prospero cannot leave until wafted away by the clapping hands and 'gentle breath' (good report) of the audience and the final chorus to *Henry V* calls it a story pursued 'Thus far' and broken off. Equally, as Robert Wilcher showed (Wilcher 1997), a number of plays use double endings, one in Act 4 and one in Act 5, as when the Duke invites everyone home to dinner after the trial in

The Merchant of Venice and Antony ends his affair with Cleopatra by killing himself.

As often as the plays present final moments of closure, of 'dwindling' into mundanity, they insist on subverting our expectations: two endings or three or none at all. This formal characteristic of Shakespeare's drama bears upon a Marxist understanding of how the plays represent inevitability since it presents opportunities for open-endedness, for Brecht's sense of other possibilities only just failing to come about. An anti-teleology resides within that most predictable of outcomes, a Shakespearian ending. This combination of predictability and surprise is a function of Shakespeare's writing and the subsequent uses of it. Being the most widely taught, read, and performed dramatic works in history, Shakespeare's plays above all others have outcomes an audience is likely to know in advance, so the surprises in a particular performance or reading emerge *despite* this familiarity. Performers and critics are under an intense pressure to find new ways with old texts, and this above all else makes Shakespeare the primary place where a Marxist sense of the tension between inevitability and the human powers of intervention can be expressed in art.

4

Shakespeare and Marx Today

Marxism is not a magical key that unlocks Shakespeare. It is an approach to economic realities, ideas, language, and art in all its forms that draws on the concepts and principles we have been discussing (such as ideology, dialectics, exchange, alienation, commodity fetishism, and reification) and can connect Shakespeare's historical, cultural, and intellectual context with the imaginative works he produced. It is not simply a matter of 'following the money', for much of what we have seen has drawn on philosophical, historical, and psychological works, and the readings offered here are intended to suggest the wide range of things a Marxist approach can attend to. They are necessarily disparate and discontinuous, united only by an attempt to show the various Marxist concepts and principles in their practical roles within Shakespeare criticism.

Property, Inflation, and Social Bonds: *The Merchant of Venice* and *Timon of Athens*

By the middle of November 1923 an American dollar was worth over 4.2 trillion German marks and rising by the hour. This had little direct effect on the rich, whose wealth was embodied in real land, buildings, and portables, or on the poor, who owned little or nothing. Those whose limited wealth was in the bank, however, were devastated by hyper-inflation as a life's work recorded on a ledger sheet was effectively erased. In industrial capitalism the middle class is normally quiescent, but hyper-inflation turns sober professionals into radicals, and in Weimar Germany the political middle ground disappeared and street battles between communists and Nazis became increasingly common. Currency reform stabilized the economy and forestalled revolution, but the crisis was essentially repeated in the depression that followed the New York stock market crash of 1929. As support for the communists rose, the German bourgeoisie chose to support the declining Nazi party rather than face revolution and Hitler was given the chancellorship. The outcome for Europe's Jews—and its communists, disabled, Roma, and homosexuals—is well known.

Although not of the scale seen in the twentieth century, the 1590s were also a period of high inflation in England, driven in part by crop failures in the middle years of the decade (Williams 1995, 160–3). In times of inflation, hoarding money is a sure way to lose it, and Scott Cutler Shershow has argued that in *The Merchant of Venice* Shakespeare contrasted pre-capitalist hoarding by Shylock with the new capitalist activism that puts money into circulation, as when Jessica 'liberates' her father's wealth and escapes the confines of his house (Shershow 2001, 259). The biblical Parable of the Talents presented a similar dilemma in this regard in its advocation of usury.

Shershow showed that our modern sense of 'talent' as an ability or skill emerged from this dilemma (see p. 33): making the 'talents' abstract qualities rather than concrete units of currency allowed for a figural interpretation that avoids the taint of usury (Shershow 2001, 252–4). From our perspective capitalism might seem a kind of hoarding inasmuch as huge wealth is kept in fewer and fewer hands, but Marx insisted that in its infancy capitalism was a freeing-up of productive forces; only later did it become a fetter on production. Both perspectives can be expressed in the verb 'to thrive', which in Bassanio's mouth means profit-making: 'I have a mind presages me such thrift' (1.1.175) and 'Here do I choose, and thrive I as I may' (2.7.60). Shylock uses this sense too—'my well-won thrift—/ Which he calls interest', 'This was a way to thrive', 'thrift is blessing, if men steal it not' (1.3.48–9, 88–9)—but he also uses it in Hamlet's sense of careful avoidance of household loss ('Thrift, thrift, Horatio. The funeral baked meats / Did coldly furnish forth the marriage tables', 1.2.179–80). Shylock worries about leaving his house in the care of the 'unthrifty knave' Lancelot (1.3.175) and cautions Jessica to lock up securely: 'Fast bind, fast find—/ A proverb never stale in thrifty mind' (2.5.53–4).

Another biblical parable running through *The Merchant of Venice* is the Prodigal Son (Luke 15:11–32). Bassanio admits to prodigality when making his initial request to Antonio (1.1.129) and Shylock accuses Antonio of it as he goes to eat with the Christians (2.5.15). Anticipating Lorenzo's arrival to take Jessica from her father's house, Graziano uses the before-and-after image of the Prodigal Son leaving home in splendour and returning in disgrace for Lorenzo's likely cooling-off after enjoying sex with Jessica (2.6.8–19). One of the play's marked indeterminacies is the degree to which this prediction is realized in performance, for the tone of Lorenzo and Jessica's catalogue of un-happy lovers at the beginning of the final act can, in different perform-ances, vary from playful banter to world-weary cynicism, and Lorenzo might be referring to himself when he accuses Jessica of running 'with an unthrift love' from Venice (5.1.16). Although self-evidently about money, its preservation and multiplication, the play overlays this with matters of class and religion that Marxism illuminates.

Class distinctions first arise not in relation to people but to ships, when Salerio imputes Antonio's sadness to anxiety about his ventures at sea:

> There where your argosies with portly sail,
> Like signors and rich burghers on the flood—
> Or as it were the pageants of the sea—
> Do overpeer the petty traffickers
> That curtsy to them, do them reverence,
>
> (1.1.9–13)

The ships of the 'royal merchant', as Graziano and the duke call Antonio (3.2.237 and 4.1.28), are imagined as portly gentlemen—or perhaps only prosperous citizens ('burghers')—lording it over their lessers. Were it meant to cheer Antonio, what follows (1.1.24–34) must surely fail for Salerio and Solanio conjure three natural shocks that fleets are heir to: 'a wind too great ... shallows and ... flats, / And ... dangerous rocks'. By these means might pomp be brought down ('her hightop lower than her ribs / To kiss her burial') and the delights of the dainty made common: 'scatter all her spices on the stream, / Enrobe the roaring waters with my silks'. In its opening moments, then, the play imagines the deflation of overblown egos and the destruction of privately held wealth.

It is not easy to determine the social status of the young men of Venice, and Antonio's reference to their 'business' (1.1.63) did not necessarily evoke 'trade', a distinct sense first recorded about 120 years after this play (*OED* business *n.* 21a). Bassanio freely admits to inflating the appearance of his social standing, for which he uses the same language of puffiness as Salerio: 'showing a more swelling port' (1.1.124). Maintaining this inflated presentation has already drained Antonio's resources when Bassanio suggests further expense on a speculative venture—about fleece rather than fleets, as Salerio later puns (3.2.240)—that will recover its own outlay and the previously squandered money. In the economics of financial speculation a key dilemma is when to cut one's losses and pull out of a falling market, and Bassanio's anecdote about 'shoot[ing] another arrow that self way / Which you did shoot the first' (1.1.148–9) in order to recover both inventively pre-empts the obvious objection that this would be 'good money after bad'. Shylock later faces the same dilemma in seeking to recover what Jessica stole: 'the thief gone with so much, and so much to find the thief' (3.1.86–7).

Even Lancelot puffs himself up. 'Talk you of young Master Lancelot', he asks his father (2.2.44), using the title reserved for, at the least, citizens free of a livery company and able to indenture apprentices. Equally deceptive, but in the opposite direction, is the stage business of spreading his fingers across his chest (to simulate ribs for his blind father to feel) that often accompanies Lancelot's 'I am famished in his [Shylock's] service. You may tell every finger I have with my ribs' (2.2.100–1). He means, presumably, you may tell (count) every one of my ribs with your finger, although possibly 'every finger' means 'every opportunity to steal' (*OED* finger *n.* 3b), and his protruding ribs show that Shylock's tight control over his household consumables has curtailed the traditional liberties of service.

Oddly, the play's one undeniably wealthy character is told by her waiting woman that her sickness comes from having too much and that it is 'no mean happiness, therefore, to be seated in the mean' (1.2.7– 8). Nerissa here invokes the distinct meanings of the homonyms 'mean' (inferior) and 'mean' (middling) that have 'mixed ancestry' (*OED* mean *a.*¹ and *adv.*¹) because the middling is a position that can be disparaged by those above. In Belmont male suitors are evaluated by their habits and appearance and Bassanio is described as 'a scholar and a soldier' (1.2.110), ancient and venerable occupations that nothing else in the play confirms.

Determining someone's occupation and class by their appearance was much easier for Elizabethans than for us because, until they were repealed (virtually by accident) in 1604, English sumptuary laws regulated what could be worn by members of each social class (Hunt 1996, 295–324). One could always dress down, of course, and the laws were expressly intended to limit dressing up: none could wear satin in their gowns, cloaks, or coats, for example, except knights' eldest sons (and above) and those with a net income of at least £100. Apart from Lancelot, the Christians of Venice seem to be gentlemen of some kind, although there is a gradation apparent in Graziano's servile relationship to Bassanio mirroring Portia's to Nerissa and perhaps also in Lancelot's being given 'a livery / More guarded [ornamented] than his fellows' (2.1.159–60).

However, running against this old-fashioned rank-order, and (in England at least) its clear representation in a hierarchy of clothing, is the knowledge-based economy of mercantile Venice in which information about the fortunes of a man's cargo in a ship many miles away matters more than whatever he happens to be wearing now. The cry for information, 'What news on the Rialto?', is used by Shylock (1.3.36) and Solanio (3.1.1) and although Shylock does not seem to recognize Antonio he gives the fellow businessman's usual hailing:

> *Enter Antonio*
> [SHYLOCK] [*To Antonio*] What news on the Rialto? [*To Bassanio*]
>   Who is he comes here?
> BASSANIO This is Signor Antonio.
>
> (1.3.36–8)

Shylock is in fact well informed about Antonio's affairs, and shipping information appears to flow freely on the Rialto:

> [SHYLOCK] Yet his means are in supposition. He hath an argosy bound to Tripolis, another to the Indies. I understand moreover upon the Rialto he hath a third at Mexico, a fourth for England, and other ventures he hath squandered abroad.
>
> (1.3.17–21)

Shylock's valuation of Antonio counts only his ships at sea, as though he had nothing else. Indeed, Antonio told Salerio and Solanio that he had other wealth not at risk (1.1.43–4) but to Bassanio he admits that this was a lie: 'all my fortunes are at sea' (1.1.177).

Information flows between Jewish and Christian merchants and Solanio makes the habitual 'What news?' enquiry even as Shylock enters in his rage concerning Jessica's flight (3.1.22). Now knowledge loses its ethical neutrality: 'SHYLOCK You knew, none so well, none so well as you, of my daughter's flight' (3.1.23–4). News floods into this scene from different quarters and about different matters. It is 'unchecked' (that is, uncontradicted) on the Rialto that Antonio has lost a cargo on the Goodwin sands (3.1.4), while from Genoa Shylock hears of Antonio's misfortune and his daughter's profligacy.

These things are not necessarily true: Salerio qualifies his account with 'if my gossip Report be an honest woman of her word' (she often is not, in Shakespeare) and in the final scene Antonio receives news that three of his cargoes are safely harboured, so Salerio's 'confirmation' that 'Not one' escaped shipwreck (3.2.269) and Antonio's 'all miscarried' (3.2.313–14) are clearly misreportings. The power and also the vulnerability of the information economy come from its reliance on confidence: Antonio's good 'credit' (1.1.180), from the Latin 'credere' (to trust, believe), gets him into the deal with Shylock, just as Portia's entirely credible impersonation of a lawyer gets him out of it.

What Belsey called 'the idealist tendency to analyse love and ignore money' (Belsey 1991, 258) is not possible with *The Merchant of Venice* because the play entangles them with bonds of support and dependence. Old Gobbo calls his son Lancelot 'the very staff of my age, my very prop' (2.2.62–3) just as Shylock likens the means by which he lives (his capital) to 'the prop / That doth sustain my house' (4.1.372–3); neither stands unsupported. The court case turns on the nature of property: is it possible for Shylock to own a pound of Antonio's flesh?

Shylock's court-room argument is that since Venice permits the keeping of slaves it has already accepted the principle that flesh can be owned. The court upholds this principle and accepts Shylock's claim—'A pound of that same merchant's flesh is thine' (4.1.296)—but punishes him for acting to enforce this claim since it is a crime for an alien to 'seek the life of any citizen' (4.1.348). The pound of flesh, then, has already been alienated from the rest of the citizen who formerly owned it (but lost it by a contractual forfeit), and what catches Shylock is the act of trying to separate his property from

Antonio's. However, this property itself contains something Shylock does not own, the blood inside the flesh's veins and arteries.

Portia demands that Shylock take only what is his:

> If thou tak'st more
> Or less than a just pound, be it but so much
> As makes it light or heavy in the substance
> Or the division of the twentieth part
> Of one poor scruple—nay, if the scale do turn
> But in the estimation of a hair,
> Thou diest, and all thy goods are confiscate.
>
> (4.1.323–9)

It is not certain whether the width or the weight of a hair is meant here, but in a parallel usage by Falstaff it is the latter: 'the weight of a hair will turn the scales' (2 *Henry IV* 2.4.255–6). The word 'scruple' comes from the Latin 'scrupulus', meaning a small rough or hard pebble that came to be a standard unit in the apothecaries' weight system in which it comprised twenty grains, so Portia might just as easily have said 'one grain'. However, a scruple is also a thought that troubles the mind, 'esp[ecially] one...which causes a person to hesitate where others would be bolder to act' (*OED* scruple *n.*[2] 1), and this suits Portia's entrapment, for Shylock's crime against the Alien Statute is his being about to take the forfeit, but of course it is essential that he does not.

Creating for Shylock an anxiety of minuteness resulting from division upon division is Portia's ingenious solution to the Christians' problem and it is the flipside of an inflationary mathematics that has signally failed. As Peter Holland noted (Holland 2001), Christians and Jews are quick with their multiplication tables, from Portia's wish that she were 'trebled twenty times myself, / A thousand times more fair, ten thousand times more rich' (3.2.153–4) to her 'Double six thousand, and then treble that' to pay off Shylock rather than have Antonio 'lose a hair' (3.2.298–300). A hair representing the smallest part of a person that could be harmed was proverbial (Dent 1981, H26.1), but for Shakespeare human hair was also an image for near-infinite multiplicity ('Had I as many sons as I have hairs', *Macbeth*, 5.11.14) and for unity-in-multiplicity (singular 'hair' composed of many 'hairs') that may break down in time of stress, as with Hamlet's 'each particular hair to stand on end' (1.5.19).

Shylock reputedly swore to reject 'twenty times the value of the sum' he is owed (3.2.285) and in the court he asserts that even if every one of 6,000 ducats 'Were in six parts, and every part a ducat' (4.1.85), he would not accept them instead of his forfeit. Shylock rightly thinks of multiplication as a form of division (strictly, it is division of the inverse, since A times B is the same as A divided by B^{-1}), which is in keeping with Shakespeare's sense of hair as both singularity and near-infinitude. Portia's wealth is virtually infinite: as Holland noted, 3,000 ducats is so much money that even Shylock cannot lay his hands on it right away, yet Portia offers 60,000 ducats (3.2.304–5), which Holland reckoned to be about £5.4 million in modern money (Holland 2001, 16, 25). The play's Venetian ducats were 'almost certainly gold' (Holland 2001, 24), as is Portia's hair, providing an appropriate link between the main images of wealth in the play: her 'sunny locks' are a 'golden fleece' (1.1.169–70).

In the information economy of commercial Venice, value is a datum on a ledger or a word on the Rialto. Shylock's 'merry sport' (1.3.144) re-establishes the link between monetary value and material life, insisting on their real inextricability. In capitalism money tends to become an invisible medium for the exchange of data about credit worthiness, and improving technologies (coins, notes, telegraphy, and magnetic-stripe cards) have accelerated this dematerialization. The German hyper-inflation of the 1920s and '30s temporarily reversed this dematerialization in the absurdity of wheeling a barrow of banknotes to buy a loaf of bread. In such moments the conventions underlying monetary transactions are, as a Russian Formalist would quickly point out (pp. 51–3 above), defamiliarized, and the incommensurability of a pile of paper (which one cannot eat) and a loaf of bread (which one can) illustrates Marx's distinction between exchange-value and use-value.

The play is set in a city utterly dependent on exchange. Shakespeare shows that economics (the base), and not city-state politics or ethics, controls the legality (the superstructure) of Venice:

> ANTONIO
>> The Duke cannot deny the course of law,
>> For the commodity that strangers have
>> With us in Venice, if it be denied,
>> Will much impeach the justice of the state,

> Since that the trade and profit of the city
> Consisteth of all nations.
>
> (3.3.26–31)

Business makes the law. The fetishization of commodities is revealed by Shylock's bond, for the pound of flesh is exactly equivalent to the 3,000 ducats it is exchanged for, yet it has no use-value to Shylock, as he insists when suggesting the bond (1.3.162–6) and as the Christians remind him when he threatens to take it (3.1.47–8, 4.1.39–41). However, the flesh has inordinate use-value to Antonio.

The laws of Venice allow flesh to be treated as a commodity, and thus Shylock can invoke the principle of slave-ownership to argue for his ownership of part of Antonio. Capitalism did not achieve its full development until slave-ownership was abolished and the market in human flesh replaced by a market in its derivative, labouring power. To the Marxist critic questions about the character of Shylock, the wrongs we are to believe were done him and the justice of his revenge against the hypocritical Christians, are no more central to the play than Shakespeare's exploration of the economic principles of burgeoning capitalist culture.

No slaves are visible in Shakespeare's Venice, although the arguments of the court scene are hinged on their existence. An educated Elizabethan would have known that ancient Athens was a slave-owning society, although Shakespeare never shows slaves there either. However, he does place a dozen distinctly named *servants* in his *Timon of Athens*, far more than in any other of his plays, and revisits, to refine, some ideas about the nature of property and its effects on the human mind that appear in *The Merchant of Venice*.

Much like Antonio, Timon is a giver: in the first scene he relieves the imprisoned debtor Ventidius (1.1.96–110) and gives Lucilius money to enable his marriage (1.1.123–51). However, where Antonio seems particular in his largesse—endangering himself only for Bassanio—Timon gives indiscriminately and has acquired a reputation for repaying with absurdly inflated gestures the small gifts given to him:

> [SENATOR]
> If I want gold, steal but a beggar's dog
> And give it Timon, why, the dog coins gold.
> If I would sell my horse and buy twenty more

> Better than he, why, give my horse to Timon—
> Ask nothing, give it him—it foals me straight,
> And able horses. No porter at his gate,
> But rather one that smiles and still invites
> All that pass by.
>
> (2.1.5–12)

This is more than passingly like Shylock's use of an image of reproducing 'woolly breeders' (1.3.82) for the inflationary increase of money by putting it to use: '[SECOND LORD] no gift to him / But breeds the giver a return exceeding / All use of quittance' (1.1.281–3). Between Antonio and Bassanio there is at least a discussion of the return of the money, with interest, but when an improvement in Ventidius's fortunes makes him offer double the 5 talents back, Timon insists that because it was a gift not a loan it cannot be reciprocated: 'I gave it freely ever, and there's none / Can truly say he gives if he receives' (1.2.9–10).

Timon's indiscriminate generosity quickly undermines itself. Unable to pay the creditors who advanced him the money he has been giving away, Timon must put them off with: 'repair to me next morning' (2.2.26). It is not clear what good a day's grace will do Timon, unless we suppose that Athenian hyper-inflation would wipe out the value of his debt. Curiously, the amounts Timon lends and seeks to borrow do rise remarkably as the action develops. Three and 5 talents save Lucilius and Ventidius in the first scene, 50 talents are to be sought from each of three private 'friends' in order to satisfy Timon's creditors (2.2.182–9), while the state is asked for 1,000 talents, and in the event Timon's need is expressed to Lucius as 5,500 talents (3.2.29).

Terence Spencer thought that Shakespeare perhaps began the play not knowing how much a talent was and only partially corrected the amounts once he found out, and hence the repeated reference to 'so many talents' (3.2.12, 24, 37), which Spencer understood to be a placeholder that Shakespeare 'intended to fill in later' (Spencer 1953, 77). On the other hand, the variations can also be explained by Thomas Middleton's composition of part of the play, for he tended to use much larger numbers of talents in his writing than Shakespeare did (Shakespeare 2004, pp. 45–53).

Denied relief by his 'friends', Timon turns misanthropic and becomes somewhat like Apemantus, who is cynical in the precise sense of imputing bad motives to seemingly sincere acts; Apemantus was the first to see through Timon's 'friends' (1.2.39–48). Although the word 'Cynic' does not appear in the play, Apemantus is clearly an adherent of the philosophy most famously espoused by Antithenes's pupil Diogenes, who is dramatized in John Lyly's play *Campaspe*, one of Shakespeare's minor sources. 'Cynic' is a transliteration of the Greek word κυνικός meaning 'dog-like,' which the *OED* records as a popular but erroneous etymology, the true origin of the name of the 'Cynic' sect being κυνόσαργες, a gymnasium where Antisthenes taught (*OED* cynic *n.* 1).

The erroneous etymology reflects a powerful symbolism (Cynics snarl at the rest of us), and Apemantus is repeatedly called a dog, although as William Empson pointed out the dog-image does double duty as a symbol of fawning but also of admirable criticism of human weakness, as found in the sententiae of Jaques, Hamlet, and Iago (Empson 1951, 176). Shakespeare learnt from Erasmus, Empson pointed out, that even in fawning a dog is sincere and faithful, and Empson uncovered a strain of dog praising in *Timon of Athens* that Caroline Spurgeon overlooked in her quantitative account (Spurgeon 1935, 195–9). A Cynic necessarily denies all social bonds but although Timon leaves Athens to live unaided in the wilderness, Apemantus makes a distinction between his own Cynicism and Timon's misanthropy: 'This is in thee a nature but infected, /A poor unmanly melancholy, sprung / From change of fortune' (4.3.203–5).

Apemantus takes offence at Timon's emulation ('Men report / Thou dost affect my manners' 4.3.199–200), primarily because Timon's is not a philosophically motivated self-loathing but a hatred of others for what they did to him: 'If thou didst put this sour cold habit on / To castigate thy pride, 'twere well; but thou / Dost it enforcedly' (4.3.240–2). There follows a comic battle as each seeks to show the superiority of his misanthropy, Timon taking the line that only those who have been Fortune's favourite can have an authentic sense of the misery of loss. This becomes a dramatic stalemate with a genuine intellectual point, for their shared misanthropic principles prevent them admitting that they have anything in common. Just as anarchists must, on principle, resist the tyranny of even the loosest hierarchical organization that might further their political ends—merely forming a subcommittee to get a banner printed entails countless painful compromises with the evils of delegation—so the philosophical tenets of

Cynicism prevent its adherents sharing the rare pleasure of meeting a fellow believer.

Real sociability was for Marx one of the expected benefits of communism, since 'only in community...is personal freedom possible' (Marx and Engels 1974, 83). Lest this be thought a kind of Orwellian double-think, it should be noted that Marx meant that in capitalist culture 'freedom' entails the absence of constraints but also the absence of security: one is free to be at the mercy of chance. Only when class has been abolished will each of us be able to enter into combination with others as an individual rather than as an averaged class-member, whereas at the moment each person's individuality is founded on a class antagonism, although the capitalist might not notice it until, like Timon, she falls. The proletarian, of course, knew this all along.

Before his disaster Timon thinks he has a kind of communist security, and he values the fellow-feeling that bonds of reciprocity generate:

We are born to do benefits; and what better or properer can we call our own than the riches of our friends? O, what a precious comfort 'tis to have so many like brothers commanding one another's fortunes!

(1.2.98–102)

However, Timon's gift-giving does not create real bonds of reciprocity, and Shakespeare had already made fun of gift-giving with the ring business in *The Merchant of Venice*. A recognizably modern legal profession came into being in the later Roman Empire when the fiction that a lawyer received only gifts (and so was not financially interested in the verdict) was abandoned, but payment to lawyers long retained an awkward position between real and symbolic value. Bassanio claims that he will not part with the ring because it is worthless but as something given him by Portia it is inordinately valuable. That Portia-as-Balthasar demands it back again closes the circuit of gift-exchange in that play, and so permits a comic ending of sorts, whereas in *Timon of Athens* the circuit is purposely left unclosed in order to explore what tragedy ensues.

There is now virtually no way to approach the anti-Semitism of *The Merchant of Venice* without considering the Nazis' attempt to destroy European Jewry, which itself must be understood in relation to the late development of democracy and nationhood in Germany. The young Germany of the late-nineteenth century was the first state to develop a modern welfare system, one of whose peculiarities is the maintenance of a class of unemployed for whom unproductive time turns into money, although vast amounts of the former must be idled through before a modicum of the latter arrives.

Usury achieves the same kind of magical transformation and at a much faster rate, and according to Alcibiades the Athenian senate, like Timon's creditors (2.2.89–91), are usurers (3.6.104–7). 'The future comes apace', warns Flavius (2.2.145), and for usurers, as for welfare recipients, time is money. The dematerialization of goods into good words is not reversible without social bonds, and bereft of goods human beings are but bodies. Here, as in *The Merchant of Venice*, a reconnection with sociability is figured through a cut human body and the subdivision of parts to meet a multiplied debt:

> TIMON Cut my heart in sums.
> TITUS' SERVANT Mine fifty talents.
> TIMON
> Tell out my blood.
> LUCIUS' SERVANT Five thousand crowns, my lord.
> TIMON
> Five thousand drops pays that. What yours? And yours?
> VARRO'S FIRST SERVANT My lord—
> VARRO'S SECOND SERVANT My lord—
> TIMON
> Tear me, take me, and the gods fall upon you. *Exit*
>
> (3.4.90–6)

In his ravings outside the walls of Athens, Timon curses it in a fantasy of broken social bonds and inverted hierarchies: 'Slaves and fools, / Pluck the grave wrinkled senate from the bench / And minister in their steads! … Bankrupts, hold fast! … Bound servants, steal!' (4.1.4–10).

While Timon's rage comes from infinitely inflated generosity and deflated expectation, Alcibiades's much colder dispute with the senators comes from their insistence on an absolute parity of crime and punishment: 'FIRST SENATOR He forfeits his own blood that spills another' (3.6.87). The soldier that Alcibiades pleads for stands accused of manslaughter and Alcibiades ingeniously argues that the man has killed many times on behalf of Athens in war: 'To kill, I grant, is sin's extremest gust, / But in defence, by mercy, 'tis most just' (3.6.54–5).

As Alcibiades insists, the Christian bar on killing is hardly compatible with the martial ethos:

> [ALCIBIADES]
> Why then, women are more valiant
> That stay at home if bearing carry it,
> And the ass more captain than the lion, the felon
> Loaden with irons wiser than the judge,
> If wisdom be in suffering.
>
> (3.6.47–51)

Christianity is not explicitly mentioned in the play, but is alluded to within explorations of philosophical principles. The biblical Parable of the Talents underlies Timon's discovery of gold while digging for roots, since, to judge from how he uses it, it must be refined and not mineral gold and hence was buried by someone. Without social connections the gold seems valueless—as Midas famously learned, you cannot eat it—but Timon finds a way to make gold serve his misanthropic ends via Alcibiades, who reports that 'The want whereof doth daily make revolt / In my penurious band.' (4.3.92–3) This revolt against revolt is a witty double negative undoing the revolution, and Timon's gold cancels the second rebellion to enable the first, so Timon's putting the gold to its right (that is, wrong) use illustrates his own susceptibility to the very contrariness that he catalogues as gold's effect: 'Thus much of this will make / Black white, foul fair, wrong right, / Base noble, old young, coward valiant' (4.3.28–30).

For Marx, this passage showed Shakespeare getting to the heart of the difference between real ownership and the debased sense of ownership on which private property is based (Marx and Engels 1974, 100–3). In a bourgeois understanding of property, something has value only if it can be exchanged for something else (can command another's labour), whereas in fact what truly belongs to each of us and marks our individuality are prized possessions that cannot be exchanged, say a worn-out coat that holds the traces of when and where we wore it. This was a subject close to Marx's heart because of his own precarious relationship with his clothes and with the pawnbrokers (Stallybrass 1998). What Timon sees in the gold he finds is an alienated power over others, but since he has rejected all social connections this power is useless until he makes a limited concession to sociability in order to begin to undermine Athenian society.

Of course, gold is not quite the same thing as modern money, as the German middle class found in the 1920s when a small amount of gold could secure the necessaries of life but vast quantities of paper money could not. Paper money constitutes a promise to deliver a known quantity of gold ('I promise to pay the bearer...', as British banknotes say) and depends upon confidence that this promise can be kept. The real scarcity of gold, on the other hand, makes it a reliable medium of exchange even though, for most human activities, it has no more inherent uses than paper. Sensing that he is hoist on his own petard, Timon counters Apemantus's assertion that outside of social relations there is 'no use for gold' with 'The best and truest, / For here it sleeps and does no hired harm' (4.3.292–3). Timon does put the gold to use, hoping to harm where previously he hoped to help. However, these extremities are indistinguishable, for as the Third Thief observes 'If he care not for 't, he will supply us easily' (4.3.406–7), and we are effectively back at the beginning of the play.

The real target of *Timon of Athens* is not money or commerce but philosophy, which howsoever faulty does achieve positive ends. Timon's encouragement of the thieves in their 'mystery' (that is, profession) actually persuades them to abandon it (4.3.452–9). Jonathan Bate argued that in *King Lear* Shakespeare indicated his preference for practical and performative goodness—little gestures and kindnesses—over theoretical goodness expressed in philosophy (Bate 2000).

However, in *Timon of Athens* Shakespeare shows good ends coming from bad philosophical means. Of course, Timon is not the perfect Cynic for he comes to accept that not everyone is self-serving:

> Forgive my general and exceptless rashness,
> You perpetual sober gods! I do proclaim
> One honest man—mistake me not, but one,
> No more, I pray—and he's a steward.
>
> (4.3.496–9)

Cynicism is contagious, and Flavius seems to catch it: 'Grant I may ever love and rather woo / Those that would mischief me than those that do!' (4.3.469–70). Yet Timon finds it hard to accept Flavius's honesty:

> But tell me true—
> For I must ever doubt, though ne'er so sure—
> Is not thy kindness subtle, covetous,
> A usuring kindness, and, as rich men deal gifts,
> Expecting in return twenty for one?

> (4.3.507–11)

Even if Flavius has no material wealth to give Timon in expectation of a larger return (as all his 'friends' had earlier), Timon worries that immaterial kindness itself might be gifted in expectation of greater return. Such a usury of the immaterial is the essence of Christianity and, as Shershow noted (Shershow 2001, 259), in a single breath the Bible eschews interest and yet promises it: 'do good, and lend, hoping for nothing again; and your reward shall be great, and ye shall be the children of the Highest' (Luke 6:35).

The medieval church courts punished usury, but a statute of 1545 permitted it where the interest rate did not exceed one-tenth of the principal. One-tenth was also the amount of agricultural produce that Mosaic law ordained should be given to support priests (Leviticus 27:30), a kind of rent on the land provided by God. Therein lay a distinction between land and all other property: 'Taking money for the use of money was often [in Shakespeare's time] viewed with distaste, but taking rent for the use of land was not considered sinful or illegal' (Sokol and Sokol 2000, 'usury/interest'). Timon formerly owned land, now lost to his creditors (2.2.142–3), and the Christian gentlemen in *The Merchant of Venice* maintain the appearance of landowning aristocrats; the lands that Shylock stands to forfeit (4.1.307) presumably came to him by the same process that lost Timon his.

The exacting of tithes was 'decimation' (from *decima*, Latin for tenth), which in another sense was the killing of one-tenth of a population for punishment, as an Athenian senator offers Alcibiades to placate his wrath:

> By decimation and a tithèd death,
> If thy revenges hunger for that food
> Which nature loathes, take thou the destined tenth,
> And by the hazard of the spotted die
> Let die the spotted.

> (5.5.31–5)

The alternative, the senators fear, is the destruction of all the citizens, so this one-tenth would be a kind of proportionate response to the wrongs that they admit Alcibiades has suffered.

Another senator dissents from this since 'All have not offended. / For those that were, it is not square to take, / On those that are, revenges', and he advocates exacting justice only upon 'those that have offended' (5.5.35–42). Here the plot of *Timon of Athens* clearly comes awry for the only injustice we have seen Alcibiades suffer was banishment for pleading against the sentencing of a manslaughtering soldier, although arguably he also comes to right Timon's wrongs. In accepting the senators' offer of a peaceful settlement, however, Alcibiades negates the very principle (that soldiers' deeds put them beyond the law) that prompted his banishment and rebellion:

> Those enemies of Timon's and mine own
> Whom you yourselves shall set out for reproof
> Fall, and no more; and to atone your fears
> With my more noble meaning, not a man
> Shall pass his quarter or offend the stream
> Of regular justice in your city's bounds
> But shall be remedied to your public laws
> At heaviest answer.

> (5.5.56–63)

Not only will Alcibiades confine his revenge to his own and Timon's enemies, but he will henceforth accept that civic law outweighs any debt that citizens might owe to soldiers.

In his final words Alcibiades appears to give up violence—'Make war breed peace, make peace stint war' (5.5.88)—but then he uses a medical image that might suggest that violence has its place: 'make each [war and peace] / Prescribe to other as each other's leech' (5.5.88–9). The principle invoked might be one of mutual benefit, as in H. J. Oliver's gloss 'as two physicians may prescribe for each other's ailments' (Shakespeare 1959, 140). Katharine Eisaman Maus offered the rather more troubling ' . . . war purges peace of its decadence, and peace purges war of its violence' (Shakespeare 1997, 2305). Ralph Berry hung a reading of the whole play on this word 'leech' that he thought 'resolves' the play, 'interprets it' as a bleak examination of the necessity of blood-letting of the body politic (Berry 1981, 101–19).

These readings miss the reciprocity implied by the image and mistake it for Timon's desperate image of mutuality, 'Be Alcibiades your plague, you his' (5.2.74). Two leeches fastening one to the other would only share blood, for what each lost it would simultaneously recover in its own feeding. The circulation of wealth that Timon thought he had initiated with his gift-giving failed because others did not reciprocate, and Alcibiades's image of mutual beneficence is the mirror image of such selfishness. Timon's miserable attempts to undermine Athens by spreading gold were virtually indistinguishable from his earlier generosity, which shows just how easily a virtuous circle may become vicious, and how it may just as easily be changed back again.

Knowing What's to Come: Historical Inevitability and *King Lear*

Unlike most of us, the first audiences at new plays by Shakespeare would not necessarily have known how the stories would end. Plays that purported to represent English history, of course, would be constrained by the events recorded in the chronicles and in popular memory, but as a genre 'history' itself was not quite as clear-cut as it was to become after the 1623 Folio's classificatory system was widely accepted. Early quarto printings of the 'history' plays often did not use that word on their title pages, and yet *The Merchant of Venice* first appeared in print as *The Most Excellent History of the Merchant of Venice* (1600).

Sometimes a story was so well known that the first audience could predict the outcome, as with *King Lear* that had circulated in a number of forms (play, prose, and poetry), all of which had the king's youngest daughter leading a French army into England, defeating her father's enemies, and restoring him to the throne. The existing play ended at that point and was printed in 1605, probably giving Shakespeare the idea for his play (Knowles 2002). Other tellings continued the narrative to the king's natural death, his daughter's succession, and a rebellion that leads to her death in prison, although this might simply form a coda to the story, as in William Warner's *Albion's England*, where the account ends with a couplet summarizing what will not be described: 'Not how her nephews war on her.../ Shall follow' (Bullough 1973, 338).

It must have come as something of a surprise, then, for the army of Shakespeare's Cordelia to fail where it had succeeded in all previous tellings, and for Lear not to be restored as expected. The genre expectations thrown up by the simplest distinction between comedy (in which no one good should die) and tragedy (in which the good must die) were already clouded by the emergence around the turn of the century of what Martin Wiggins called the hermaphrodite genre of tragicomedy (Wiggins 2000, 102–22). Thus the horrible violence in the middle of Shakespeare's *King Lear* would not have given the audience warning that, unlike the story they knew, this afternoon's entertainment was going to end unhappily. The body that Lear carries on in the final moments of the play was probably expected to recover.

Shakespeare revised *King Lear* for a revival around 1610 (Shakespeare 2000, 3–9; Taylor and Warren 1983) and amongst the changes was the insertion of a paradoxical prophecy made by the Fool that appears only in the 1623 Folio text. A modernized version of it would look like this:

This is a brave night to cool a courtesan.
I'll speak a prophecy ere I go:

When priests are more in word than matter;	
When brewers mar their malt with water;	
When nobles are their tailors' tutors,	How things stand now
No heretics burned, but wenches' suitors,	
When every case in law is right;	
No squire in debt nor no poor knight;	
When slanders do not live in tongues,	
Nor cutpurses come not to throngs;	How things might be in the
When usurers tell their gold i' th' field,	future
And bawds and whores do churches build,	
Then shall the realm of Albion	
Come to great confusion.	An outcome (disastrous)
Then comes the time, who lives to see 't,	
That going shall be used with feet.	Another outcome (proper)
This prophecy Merlin shall make; for I live	
before his time.	

(3.2.79–94)

The division into sections and the labels to the right are mine, of course. This is not how most editors represent the prophecy, however, and a brief history of their emendations will illuminate the diagnosis and prognosis of social ills, something Marxism specializes in.

In his edition of 1747 Reverend William Warburton noted that

> The judicious reader will observe through this heap of nonsense and confusion, that this is not *one*, but *two* prophecies. The first, a satyrical description of the *present manners as future*: And the second, a satyrical description *of future manners, which the corruption of the present would prevent from ever happening.* Each of these prophecies has its proper inference or deduction: yet, by an unaccountable stupidity, the first editors took the whole to be all one prophecy, and so jumbled the two contrary inferences together. (Shakespeare 1747a, 77)

Warburton was aided in seeing two prophecies because he used Alexander Pope's text (1723–5) and Pope had altered the second line to read 'or ere I go' to improve the metre, and since this 'is not English', Warburton made good the obvious 'loss of a word' by emending to 'a prophecy or two ere I go'.

To put the right outcome after each prophecy, Warburton re-ordered the lines so that what I have called 'How things stand now' was followed by the proper outcome (walking on feet) and what I have called 'How things might be in the future' was followed by the disastrous outcome. Kenneth Muir rightly observed that Warburton divided the speech into 'the actual [i.e. present] state of affairs' and a 'Utopian' state (Shakespeare 1952, 111), but the important thing is that for Warburton the Utopian was necessarily impossible, as we can tell from his labels 'Now' and 'Never' for what I have called 'now' and 'the future'. Albion, in Warburton's understanding and re-ordering of the text, can never come to confusion.

Warburton was the leading religious polemicist of the eighteenth century, an arch-enemy of deism and Catholicism and intensely interested in the role of miracles in the revelation of Christian truth. Warburton's major religious work was *The Divine Legation of Moses* (1738–41), which aimed to show the truth of Mosaic religion as a predecessor of Christianity from the evidence that, unlike its competitor religions, it offered no promise of future happiness in life after death. Those predecessor religions were merely the tools of rulers who did not believe in the afterlife but used its promise to secure acquiescence from their people, whereas the Jews had the providential intervention of God in their daily lives and needed no promises about the future. Because Moses did not exploit promises of an afterlife in the way that other religious leaders did, Christianity's subsequent promise of an afterlife was in fact a revealed truth not a manipulative ploy.

For the Oxford *Complete Works*, Stanley Wells and Gary Taylor followed George Ian Duthie and John Dover Wilson (Wells et al. 1987, 535) in reordering the speech in a different way again: 'How things stand now' they followed with the disastrous outcome, and 'How things might be in the future' they followed with the proper outcome. Duthie and Wilson's defence of this is instructive:

> We prefer our order, since it gives a couple of stanzas meaning: 'When things shall be as in fact they are, Britain will be in a state of ruin, as in fact she is; when things shall be as they should be, then walking will customarily be done with feet, i.e. the proper order will prevail, and men will walk uprightly—but no one will ever live to see this.' (Shakespeare 1960, 203)

The contrast could not be more complete between Warburton's Augustan confidence that, howsoever imperfect present human behaviour might be, Albion could never come to utter confusion, and Duthie–Wilson's post-war suspicion that it already has and can never be put right. Elsewhere, Taylor read what I call 'How things might be in the future' as 'conditions [that] could never be satisfied' (Taylor 1983, 383). Likewise, John Kerrigan understood this speech as showing the Fool's wise appreciation of 'what life is like' in a play that 'makes no concessions to what we would like life to be', but part of his evidence for the play's pessimism is the very Duthie–Wilson ordering of the parts that constructs this world-weariness in the first place (Kerrigan 1983, 225–6, 238).

Amongst the slippery matters at stake here is just what we mean by 'now' in relation to this play. There is a kind of doubleness in the Fool prophesying that Merlin will make this prophecy, and there are at least three potential 'nows' even before we consider the four centuries that separate us from the first performances: (i) the time the play is set, (ii) Merlin's time (the play's future), and (iii) the time of first performance (1605). The Fool's use of 'Albion' might alert us to the last of these, the time of performance, because this word was especially charged for the play's first audiences.

'Albion' can mean 'Great Britain' (the island containing modern-day England, Scotland, and Wales), which is the political entity that

James I had himself proclaimed king of in 1604, a name coming from the Latin word *Albus* by allusion to the white cliffs of Dover that someone travelling the shortest way from France—as Cordelia does— would see first (*OED* Albion *n.*). In Irish 'Albanach' and in Scottish 'Albannech' meant 'pertaining to Scotland' (*OED* Albanian *n.* and *a.*), so it is hard not to also hear in 'Albion', and in the character name Albany, allusions to James's Scottishness. Indeed, as Andrew Gurr pointed out, the opening line of the play ('I thought the King had more affected the Duke of Albany than Cornwall') must have been shock-ingly topical (emphasizing the 'now' of performance) when presented at court on 26 December 1606, since James's elder son had been Duke of Albany since 1601 and his young brother had just been made Duke of Cornwall (Gurr 2002, 44).

'Albion' in the Fool's prophecy is a powerfully compressed image for the intertwining of the personal and the political, familial strife in the subplot and the ambivalences of a Scottish king uniting the kingdoms of the whole island of Albion. Shakespeare's only other uses of 'Albion' are in plays explicitly offering versions of English history (*Henry V* and 2 and 3 *Henry VI*), where the kind of surprising departure from the known outcome we see in *King Lear* was not possible. Shakespeare added the Fool's speech about the future of Albion as part of a wholesale revision of the play, including changing who speaks the closing lines, and thereby enhanced the sense (as a Marxist must appreciate) of the unfixity, rather than inevitability, of historical out-comes.

In Peter Holland's reading, the final lines 'The oldest hath borne most. We that are young / Shall never see so much, nor live so long' (5.3.301–2) assert that events are unrepeatable, that '... the play has used up one of the potential narratives of the world' (Holland 1991, 55), and this makes the play like 'history', which in all its particularities never occurs more than once. However, in its generalities, history seems to repeat itself: 'Hegel says somewhere that, upon the stage of universal history, all great events and personalities reappear in one fashion or another. He forgot to add that, on the first occasion, they appear as tragedy; on the second, as farce' (Marx 1926, 23).

We have seen that one of the most influential inheritors of Marx's ideas is Jacques Derrida, and in typically self-contradictory fashion he observed that '... the singularity of any *first* time makes it also a *last* time' since it can never again be the first time (Derrida 1994, 10). This actually makes quite simple sense in relation to the surprise ending of *King Lear*, since the repertory system that prevailed in theatres of Shakespeare's time undoubtedly gave the play repeat public performances, but never again could it have the impact of the first one. Shakespeare turned comedy to tragedy when he surprised his audience with the ending of *King Lear*, and in one sense Marxism is the opposite reversal. Marxism is an inherently comedic doctrine because, ironically, it seeks to do away with itself by abolishing the conditions that gave rise to it. Like Edgar, who seems to write himself into and out of an account of what has passed ('We ... Shall never see' what he has seen), Marxism writes itself into history in order to write itself out again in the push to get real history started by ending the class struggle that holds it back.

It Isn't the Thing: The Crisis of Representation in *Hamlet*

A well-known story concerns a young man who communes with a ghost who talks only to him and who instructs him to commit a revenge murder. The story indeed ends with mass murder and along the way there is a memorable scene concerning an actor's ability to imitate intense emotions at a moment's notice. With the final clue that dark suspicions of wrongdoing are intimated by use of the phrase 'something is rotten in Denmark', you will doubtless guess that I am referring to Quentin Tarantino's script for the film *True Romance* (Scott 1993). In Shakespeare, of course, the line is 'Something is rotten in the *state* of Denmark' (1.4.67) and, as we have seen (pp. 35–6 above), in 'Ideology and Ideological State Apparatuses' Louis Althusser gave the state a central role in the formation of individual identities.

Hamlet's interest in actors and acting shares Althusser's concern for the means by which individuals' sense of who they are is formed within social parameters and for apparently authentic selfhood being a role that one has been given by society. Rejecting Gertrude's 'Why seems it [grief at death] so particular with thee?', Hamlet insists

> Seems, madam? Nay, it *is*. I know not 'seems'.
> 'Tis not alone my inky cloak, good-mother,

> Nor customary suits of solemn black,
> Nor windy suspiration of forced breath,
> No, nor the fruitful river in the eye,
> Nor the dejected haviour of the visage,
> Together with all forms, moods, shows of grief
> That can denote me truly. These indeed 'seem',
> For they are actions that a man might play;
> But I have that within which passeth show—
>
> (1.2.76–85)

The things that do not denote him 'truly' read like theatrical clichés that Hamlet rejects in favour of an inexpressible interior, 'that within'.

The great semiotician of the theatre, Umberto Eco, pointed out that showing rather than saying, or showing as well as saying, is the essence of theatre. To illustrate, Eco imagined himself being asked by a friend 'How should I be dressed for the party this evening?':

> If I answer by showing my tie framed by my jacket and say, 'Like this, more or less,' I am signifying by ostension. My tie does not mean my actual tie but your possible tie (which can be of different stuff and color) and I am 'performing' by representing to you the you of this evening. I am prescribing how you should look this evening. (Eco 1977, 110)

The phrase 'more or less' modified the act of showing, the ostension: '...[I]t helped you to de-realize the object that was *standing* for something else. It was reducing the pertinent features of the vehicle I used to signify 'tie' to you, in order to make it able to signify all the possible ties you can think of' (Eco 1977, 111). Shakespeare repeatedly returned to explorations of the way that objects on a stage can represent other objects of the same kind and how the actor inserts himself into this phenomenon.

In *True Romance* an actor called Lance auditions for a part in the television series *T. J. Hooker*, and the actor playing Lance must show that Lance is a poor actor, an uncomfortable task for anyone trying to make the most of a minor role in a film. Performed well, this bad acting might be so believable that the cinema audience will decide that the actor playing Lance is bad, rather than that he excels at imitating bad imitation. In probably his first play, *The Two Gentleman of Verona*, Shakespeare gave a servant, also called Lance, a similar problem:

Nay, I'll show you the manner of it. This shoe is my father. No, this left shoe is my father. No, no, this left shoe is my mother. Nay, that cannot be so, neither. Yes, it is so, it is so, it hath the worser sole. This shoe with the hole in it is my mother, and this my father. A vengeance on 't, there 'tis. Now, sir, this staff is my sister, for, look you, she is as white as a lily and as small as a wand. This hat is Nan our maid. I am the dog. No, the dog is himself, and I am the dog. O, the dog is me, and I am myself.

(2.3.13–23)

Assigning the roles to the various props available to him Lance's signifying project is workable, if excessively figurative. However, the dog Crab and his owner Lance were part of the scene of tearful leave-taking that Lance is trying to convey, which makes it difficult for him to decide how they should be represented. The problem is that those doing the representing are those being represented, and hence Lance traps himself in what Eco called 'the crucial antinomy that has haunted the history of western thought for two thousand years... the "liar" paradox—someone asserts that all he is telling is false' (Eco 1977, 115).

Although Althusser (following Jacques Lacan) would say that he is much too old to worry about it now, Hamlet is obsessed with not being interpellated by Danish state ideology, with not playing a role assigned to him, with remaining 'not a pipe for Fortune's finger / To sound what stop she please' (3.2.68–9), a metaphor that recurs in his outburst to Guildenstern 'do you think I am easier to be played on than a pipe?' (3.2.357–8). Yet he is mightily impressed with the effect of a performance upon the performer:

> Is it not monstrous that this player here,
> But in a fiction, in a dream of passion,
> Could force his soul so to his whole conceit
> That from her working all his visage wanned,
> Tears in his eyes, distraction in 's aspect,
> A broken voice, and his whole function suiting
> With forms to his conceit?

(2.2.553–9)

Whether Hamlet is more impressed with the actor's 'seeming' for its effect on the actor (or is it the cause?) or on the audience (himself), his pondering leads him to the idea that Claudius's response to performance of 'something like the murder' (2.2.597) of his father might reveal whether the Ghost's account is true. For his revenge Hamlet wants grounds less uncertain, less 'relative' in our modern sense of that word (dependent on something, or someone, else rather than absolute), but oddly he says he wants grounds 'More relative than this' (2.2.606).

The first editor who felt the need to explain what sense Hamlet means by 'relative' was Warburton, who gave the gloss 'convictive' (Shakespeare 1747b, 179n5), although Samuel Johnson argued that this was only a consequential sense derived from the direct meaning of 'nearly related, closely connected' (Shakespeare 1765b, 204n8). That Warburton should re-enter here is apt, for his view of how early language developed—explained in *The Divine Legation of Moses* (Warburton 1741, 66–206)—was what Derrida reacted against at the heart of his *Of Grammatology* that marked the fundamental shift in the progression of Marxist thinking after 1968. For Derrida, language—indeed, any kind of representation—cannot sustain the certainty that Hamlet seeks (Derrida 1976, 269–316).

In Warburton's account, the language of speech derived from the gestural language of action, the latter being primary, while Jean-Jacques Rousseau saw two different sources: mere 'need' produced gestural signifying while passion 'wrung forth the first words' (Derrida 1976, 273). For Rousseau, signification itself was corrupted at source because figurative language preceded literal language. This counter-intuitive claim needs explanation, and Derrida offered the example of an early human coming across another human and in her terror seeing the potential enemy as someone much larger than herself, for which she invented the signifier 'giant'. Once this had happened enough times the fear wore off and the early human invented the literal 'human' for any other individual and reserved the earlier, fear-laden, term 'giant' for metaphorical use.

While still fearful of others, 'giant' represented not what was seen (which was just another human) but the feeling of fear about what was seen, the passion inherent in the signified. However, this signified itself was not singular: it represented not only the thing seen but the passionate feeling about the thing seen, so metaphoricity had already entered into the sign at the level of the signified, which was itself a signifier of the passion. The idea 'giant' literally represented the representer of the passion, but only metaphorically represented the 'human' and only metaphorically represented the feeling: 'it is the sign of a sign . . . It represents the affect literally only through representing a false representer'; a speaker or writer 'can reproduce and calculate this operation' and so produce figurative speech or writing (Derrida 1976, 277). Thus metaphoricity exists at the heart of the sign so there are no literals: 'Il n'y a pas de hors-texte', 'there is nothing outside the text' (Derrida 1976, 158).

In hoping to catch Claudius with a theatrical representation, a stage picture, Hamlet shares Warburton's view on the primacy of the visual: 'To express the idea of a man or of a horse, they represented the form of each of these animals; so that the first essay towards writing was a mere picture' (Derrida 1976, 282; Warburton 1741, 67). And yet Hamlet refers to this performance as an aural rather than a visual event: 'We'll hear a play tomorrow' (2.2.538–9). The same phrasing occurs in *The Taming of the Shrew*: 'hear you play. . . heard a play. . . hear a play' (Induction 1.91, 94, 2.130). It is commonly asserted that in Shakespeare's time people referred to hearing a play rather than (as we do) seeing it, theirs being allegedly a more aurally based culture. In fact, almost everyone but Shakespeare referred to seeing a play but his subsequent dominance of the period has obscured this fact (Egan 2001a).

The difference between seeing something and hearing it goes to the heart of a long-standing critical debate about Hamlet's use of the play-within-the-play: why does Claudius not react to the dumb-show representation of his 'crime', only to its repetition in the performance proper (Greg 1917; Wilson 1935, 138–97; Hawkes 1986, 101–19; Bradshaw 2001)? For W. W. Greg, Claudius's innocence is proved by his not reacting to the dumb-show, John Dover Wilson thought the dumb-show just a necessary device for the theatre audience (us) to understand how *The Murder of Gonzago* will catch the conscience of the king, Terence Hawkes saw the undecideability of this matter as part of the play's wider productive self-contradiction, and Graham Bradshaw asked why, if Claudius's reaction tells Hamlet that he is guilty of murder, does it not tell the rest of the court too? After all, no one else behaves as if Claudius's guilt has been revealed at this point. The grounds Hamlet gets are indeed more relative, but in our modern sense.

Derridean undecideability, the displacement that inheres in all representation, I have likened to the Marxist dialectic. Many important things including capitalism and class society are inherently self-contradictory, so from that point of view Derrida's 'discovery' is nothing new, deconstruction is just an alternative way of describing the dialectic of existence. However, from another view the ideas could not be more distinct, for Derrida's critique goes well beyond multiple, contradictory interpretations and declares reality itself unknowable other than through textual strategies built on the shifting sands of the 'supplement'. As we have seen (pp. 82–6 above), this involves a shift from realism to its opposite, epistemological idealism.

Samuel Johnson complained of Shakespeare that 'A quibble was to him the fatal *Cleopatra* for which [Shakespeare] lost the world, and was content to lose it' (Shakespeare 1765a, B3r), and Christopher Norris observed the irony that in putting it so figuratively Johnson employed 'the very linguistic vices that [he] treats with such contempt', an inevitability according to Derrida since there is no getting away from the figurative (Norris 1985, 51). A Marxist would observe that while this is true, Johnson's point served perfectly well prior to Norris's observation: that it was self-contradictory did not invalidate Johnson's insight about Shakespeare. Indeed, arguably the observation strengthens Johnson's claim since knowing that one cannot entirely evade figuration makes it easier to distinguish between greater and lesser uses of metaphor. Derrideanism can easily flatten all distinctions so that the epistemological truisms that we cannot know everything and cannot know any particular thing entirely are deformed into a postmodern certainty that we cannot know anything. Such absolutism defeats itself, for (as we know from the Liar Paradox) if all certainties are delusional, we cannot be certain that all certainties are delusional.

Exchange and Equality in *All's Well That Ends Well* and *The Comedy of Errors*

In the second quarto text, Hamlet finds in Fortinbras an emulable model of vigorous manhood willing to fight a pointless campaign (Additional scene J, end of 4.4). In Shakespeare, secret rejection of military prowess usually comes from men too cowardly to fight, such as John Oldcastle/Falstaff in the *Henry IV* plays and Paroles in *All's Well That Ends Well*, who hypocritically extol their military prowess in over-compensation for their fear. However, in *All's Well That Ends Well* there is a new development running alongside this familiar trope: the perversion of values inherent in soldiering as an end in itself. Robin Headlam Wells argued that in 1608 Shakespeare entered the public debate about the social danger of heroic values with *Coriolanus*, which specifically engaged with the cult of chivalry surrounding young Prince Henry in order to denounce it (Wells 2000).

All's Well That Ends Well seems to share the same concern. Its major source is Novel 38 'Gilletta of Narbona' in William Painter's *The Palace of Pleasure* (Bullough 1958, 389–96), and there the war between Florence and Siena that forms the primary backdrop to Shakespeare's play is almost entirely absent. In Painter's version of the story Beltramo (Bertram) flies from his new wife towards Tuscany before he hears of the Florentine/Sienese war and he joins it having already broken from her, whereas in Shakespeare's version the war gives him an additional reason—that is, as well as his dissatisfaction with his new wife—for leaving Paris. Although Beltramo is 'willingly received, and honourably entertained' (Bullough 1958, 392), and given charge of a force of men, nothing more is heard of the war in Painter's version of the story: the outcome is not mentioned, and Beltramo does not distinguish himself in battle. The war is quite inconsequential.

Shakespeare began by making much of this war. From the first scene in Paris (1.2), the young lords of France speak of little else, the king deliberates about which side to take, a message from Austria urges him not to support Florence, and the king decides to let his young noblemen choose sides for themselves: 'freely have they leave / To stand on either part' (1.2.14–15). Before the French intervention, the war is at stalemate: 'KING The Florentines and Senois are by th'ears, / Have fought with equal fortune, and continue / A braving war' (1.2.1–3). Austria's request that France deny aid to the Florentines is presumably intended to prolong this stalemate, but in expanding the war from his source Shakespeare initially took sides, following the Florentines only.

The opening stage direction of 2.1 contains information that cannot be an aid to performance but appears to be a note by Shakespeare to himself: '*Enter the King [carried in a chair], with the two Lords Dumaine, divers young lords taking leave for the Florentine war, and Bertram and Paroles*'. Here it is not a Florentine/Sienese war, just a Florentine, and this in a stage direction with detail of no use in the theatre: one cannot act being headed somewhere. As Fredson Bowers pointed out (Bowers 1980), Shakespeare seems to be using *aides-mémoire* when breaking off composition so that he might more easily pick up the thread at a later time.

Two groups stand before the king to receive his blessing: 'KING Farewell, young lords. These warlike principles / Do not throw from you. And you, my lords, farewell. / Share the advice betwixt you' (2.1.1–3). One group represents those who will fight for Florence and the other those who will fight for Siena. Clearly, members of one group might find themselves fighting members of the other group, so the courtly entertainment of tourneying is here taken to its logical limit: in the name of 'breathing and exploit' (1.2.17) the young noblemen risk killing each other.

This has happened before. Paroles boasts of a past exploit: 'You shall find in the regiment of the Spinii one Captain Spurio, with his cicatrice, an emblem of war, here on his sinister cheek. It was this very sword entrenched it. Say to him I live, and observe his reports for me' (2.1.40–4). The name Spurio is Shakespeare's unsubtle hint that this is not exactly true, but Paroles's claim to once have fought a man who is now on the same side as these young Frenchmen must be at least plausible else he would look foolish. For these young aristocrats, the choosing of sides is not a matter of principle but whim and they kill without caring which side wins.

For the purpose of defining themselves by killing, young men like Bertram find one body as good as another. They actually live the infinite exchangeability of one person for another that ideology exists to conceal. As we saw (pp. 35–6 above), Althusser conceived of ideology as the process by which each of us is made to feel individually important although we know at a rational level that if we did not occupy our particular place in society someone else would. The essence of Helen's lesson for Bertram is that in sexual relations too one body may be exchanged for another, so that his blindness to individuation rebounds on him and he is forced to accept the difference of man and man.

The Sienese and the young Frenchmen who fight for them disappear from the play together with the ugly details of a war in which the only reported casualty is the Duke of Siena's brother whom Bertram killed 'with his own hand' (3.5.6). These are not the play's only missing persons, for the opening direction of 3.5 in the 1623 Folio (our only source) is '*Enter old widow of Florence, her daughter Violenta and*

Mariana, with other Citizens', which is odd since the widow's daughter is named Diana in the subsequent dialogue. Perhaps Shakespeare meant 'her daughter' and 'Violenta' to be two separate characters, in which case the latter is technically a ghost character, having no dialogue and no part in the action. It would be too far-fetchedly symbolic to have a silent, ghostly Violenta standing in for the unrepresented violence that the play gestures towards but will not show, but the play has another such weird parallel between dramatic practicality and its themes.

There is a confusing variation of Folio speech prefixes for the characters that editors normally reduce to First Lord Dumaine and Second Lord Dumaine. If these variations stood in a manuscript used to run the play in performance, then both Lords Dumaine, on separate occasions, play the enemy general holding Paroles prisoner. Paroles's inability to detect when one takes the place of the other resonates powerfully with Bertram's inability to differentiate between the bodies of Diana and Helen. Both instructive deceptions also resonate with the peculiarly arbitrary Florentine/Sienese war in which the young French lords are allowed to choose sides. We cannot tell how many of these productive parallels between theatrical practice and the story being told would have survived into performance, nor to what extent the practice of actors 'doubling' might have enhanced or diminished these effects. However, as with Hamlet's meditations on the effect of acting on actors and on the search for truth, the connection appears to show Shakespeare's deep concern with the mechanics and philosophy of representation itself.

Twins offer a special kind of human mirroring by which writers have explored what we think and feel about ourselves, our subjectivity. For Jacques Lacan the crucial event for development of a stable ego is an infant seeing its own reflection (in a parental eyeball, before mirrors were invented) and drawing from this unified image a false sense of its own coherence (Lacan 1977, 1–7). Althusser drew on this to argue that by an analogous process ideology creates the socialized human subject by hailing it. Being treated as subjects we learn to behave as subjects. One of Marx's greatest contributions to political economy was to overturn the bourgeois neoclassical model of behaviour in which individuals survey their options and make the best use of their time and resources; instead Marx showed that external economic forces become mirrored in individual behaviour so as to perpetuate existing economic relations. The extraction of surplus value by the capitalist necessarily results 'in reproducing the working man as a working man, and the capitalist as a capitalist' (Marx 1899, 61).

In *The Comedy of Errors*, as later in *The Merchant of Venice*, merchants whose living is the endless exchange of one commodity for another come to experience that process enacted on themselves. Like Antonio, Antipholus of Ephesus starts the play a sad merchant of good credit (as reported at 5.1.6, 45), although it is his father (rather than himself) who is to die for want of money, and the merchant Balthasar is reported sad too (3.1.19). Like Venice, the world of *The Comedy of Errors* is a slave-owning economy and Egeon reports that he bought the Dromios from their 'exceeding poor' parents in order to have them attend his sons (1.1.56–7). Nothing could appeal more to a merchant than a pair of human beings from which, like his commodities, all particularities are absent: human reproduction made pure repetition. Egeon's own twins 'could not be distinguished but by names' (1.1.52), and in denying them even this distinction (calling them both Antipholus) the comic potential for the play's events was generated. Names, of course, are social phenomena, and since the boys who ended up in Ephesus were split from their parents before they could know their own names, the play is necessarily predicated on an asocial idea about language: impossibly, their names stuck to them.

Of all the things one can name the most peculiar is oneself, for as Mikhail Bakhtin observed the pronoun 'I' is unlike any other signifier in that the signified is not available for viewing, as is the object signified by, say, the word 'tree' (Holquist 1990, 27). The 'I' signified is created by imagining what it would be like to see ourselves as others see us and this is a process of authorship since we cannot actually *be* another person seeing us but must imagine that we are. Since perception is determined by the life experiences of the perceiver, our own experiences determine the process of construction of an imaginary self. We may try to see ourselves as a Martian would see us, but our view of what a Martian is like—the prerequisite for constructing the Martian who views us—is determined by our past experiences. As Marx insisted, we need others' perceptions in order to know who we are.

In *Troilus and Cressida* Ulysses and Achilles discuss the proposition that one 'Cannot make boast to have that which he hath, / Nor feels not what he owes, but by reflection—/ As when his virtues, shining upon others, / Heat them, and they retort that heat again / To the first givers' (3.3.93–7), and in *Julius Caesar* Cassius flatters Brutus with the lamenting 'That you have no such mirrors as will turn / Your hidden worthiness into your eye, / That you might see your shadow' (1.2.58–60).

It seems that Antipholus of Ephesus's other half (his wife, not his brother) used to provide this mirroring function until he began to frequent the Courtesan's house:

> ADRIANA
> Ay, ay, Antipholus, look strange and frown:
> Some other mistress hath thy sweet aspects.
> I am not Adriana, nor thy wife.
> The time was once when thou unurged wouldst vow
> That never words were music to thine ear,
> That never object pleasing in thine eye,
> That never touch well welcome to thy hand,
> That never meat sweet-savoured in thy taste,
> Unless I spake, or looked, or touched, or carved to thee.
> How comes it now, my husband, O how comes it
> That thou art then estrangèd from thyself?—
> Thy 'self' I call it, being strange to me
> That, undividable, incorporate,
> Am better than thy dear self's better part.
>
> (2.2.113–26)

What she thinks is alienation ('I am not ... thy wife') is, of course, literally true because he is not Antipholus of Ephesus but the other one, so the characters being twinned allows her to speak an absolute truth while meaning only a subjunctive one: if you change, I change. The Courtesan's business operates by commodity exchange (one paying customer is as good as another) that runs counter to the principle of two-in-one-fixity in marriage, and in case we do not get this point Shakespeare has her, merchant-like, exchange the expensive chain that would tie husband to wife for a ring of equal value. The barely submerged filthy joke, here and at the end of *The Merchant of Venice*, is that prostitutes and wives know what their 'rings' (vaginas) are worth.

For the visitors to Ephesus, the necessary detour through other people that our subjectivity must take for us to know ourselves is magnified to an unbearable degree: '[ANTIPHOLUS OF SYRACUSE] If everyone knows us, and we know none, / 'Tis time, I think, to trudge, pack, and be gone' (3.2.158–9). Unless Shakespeare is simply trying to suggest that his feelings are superficial, the fact that Antipholus of Syracuse wishes to be gone despite having just fallen in love with Luciana speaks of the powerful need for sociability to be reciprocal. More likely, the amorous feelings are in considerable tension with the real asociability of a world in which one's place is entirely carved out before one entered it, as though Althusserian interpellation was utterly constraining and ideology ignored one's refusal to acknowledge its hailing.

Certainly, Antipholus of Syracuse feels himself divided by these forces: '[Luciana] Hath almost made me traitor to myself. / But lest myself be guilty to self-wrong, / I'll stop mine ears against the mermaid's song' (3.2.168–70). Potentially, with the play's confusions ended, Luciana and Antipholus of Syracuse can offer one another the mediated selfhood that Adriana and Antipholus of Ephesus used to, although the breakdown of the latter's relationship scarcely promises a happy future.

However, the play does not end with the couples, but with the slaves, and they demonstrably can be one another's mirror: '[DROMIO OF EPHESUS] I see by you I am a sweet-faced youth' (5.1.421). Moreover, they contemplate internalizing the external system of hierarchy by age (the first born being senior) but decide against it: 'We came into the world like brother and brother, / And now let's go hand in hand, not one before another' (5.1.429–30). By contrast Emilia made her preference known long before ('My wife, more careful for the latter-born' 1.1.78), but perhaps only in response to primogeniture that would make the eldest son—even if only by a few minutes—necessarily his father's inheritor. And yet even in this the boys are exchangeable, for Egeon goes to claim contrariwise that his 'youngest boy' stayed with him until adulthood and then went in search of his elder brother (1.1.124–9).

As with *All's Well That Ends Well* this seeming accident of composition resonates with the play's egalitarian theme, and the play's final words ('not one before another') and its hand-in-hand exit insist that even though their entrance to their world could not have been simultaneous, and hence society's rules of precedence make them unequal, their departure from the stage can be simultaneous and equal.

Class and Honour in *The Winter's Tale*

One of Shakespeare's last plays, *The Winter's Tale*, tackles social change (especially regarding class) head-on, and offers a mechanism for resolving the tensions that undoubtedly increased over the two decades of his dramatic career. Importuning Camillo to conceal nothing about Leontes's sudden change of behaviour, Polixenes describes his social class:

> Camillo,
> As you are certainly a gentleman, thereto
> Clerk-like experienced, which no less adorns
> Our gentry than our parents' noble names,
> In whose success we are gentle:
>
> (1.2.390–4)

Stating that he is 'certainly a gentleman' throws into question Camillo's social station—if it were certain, there would be no need to assert it—and having 'clerk-like' experience suggests a 'keeper of accounts' (*OED* clerk *n.* senses 4, 5, and 6).

Amongst Camillo's duties is guardianship of 'The keys of all the posterns' (1.2.464), the small exits from the city, but Leontes speaks of more personal services:

> I have trusted thee, Camillo,
> With all the near'st things to my heart, as well
> My chamber-counsels, wherein, priest-like, thou
> Hast cleansed my bosom, I from thee departed
> Thy penitent reformed.
>
> (1.2.237–41)

Whatever they are, these are transferrable skills, for Camillo develops a similarly close relationship with his new master:

[POLIXENES]
  Thou, having made me businesses which none without thee can sufficiently manage, must either stay to execute them thyself or take away with thee the

very services thou hast done; which if I have not enough considered—as too much I cannot—to be more thankful to thee shall be my study, and my profit therein, the heaping friendships.

(4.2.13–20)

By 'businesses' something like commercial ventures, requiring new and specialized skills, seems implied. The first certain use of 'business' to mean trade is by Daniel Defoe in 1727 (*OED* business *n*. 21), but this does not preclude Shakespeare using the more generic term (as it was then) to denote activities that other evidence suggests were commercial: Camillo is specifically called 'clerk-like', has risen from a low-birth to a position of importance on the strength of his personal merits, and performs services for the crown that no one else is able to 'sufficiently manage'.

Camillo sounds like a kind of bourgeois agent, and while Polixenes appears comfortable with his rise, Leontes uses a couple of phrases that suggest he might not be. Leontes couches his accusation against Hermione as a collapse of all social hierarchical distinction:

> O, thou thing,
> Which I'll not call a creature of thy place
> Lest barbarism, making me the precedent,
> Should a like language use to all degrees,
> And mannerly distinguishment leave out
> Betwixt the prince and beggar.

(2.1.84–9)

Leontes's sexual doubts are inextricably bound with his doubts about his political power, expressed first in overblown assertion of unlimited scope:

> Why, what need we
> Commune with you of this, but rather follow
> Our forceful instigation? Our prerogative
> Calls not your counsels . . .
> We need no more of your advice. The matter,
> The loss, the gain, the ord'ring on 't, is all
> Properly ours.

(2.1.163–72)

This puffed-up confidence depends on the approval it denies: '[LEONTES] Have I done well?/A LORD Well done, my lord' (2.1.189–90).

Between Perdita's loss and her restoration the play is concerned almost entirely with events in rural Bohemia, where she is at the centre of a celebration of agricultural plenitude. Blessed with the Sicilian entrepreneur Camillo and the Sicilian heir, Bohemia thrives while Sicilia becomes sterile, its monarch refusing to remarry. On greeting Florizel, Leontes makes clear the allegory of seasonal renewal by exclaiming 'Welcome hither, / As is the spring to th' earth!' (5.1.150–1). What distinguishes Bohemia seems a freedom to play with social mobility: Perdita dresses up for the sheep-shearing feast—with some qualms, it is true—while Florizel, Polixenes, and Camillo dress down.

These are only pretences, but there have been real movements too in Bohemia: Camillo's rise and Autolycus's fall: 'I have served Prince Florizel, and in my time wore three-pile, but now I am out of service' (4.3.13–14). John Pitcher suggested that this is simply a 'bare-faced lie' that would have been greeted with 'laughter and catcalls from the audience in the Globe' (Pitcher 2003, 258–9)—if so it is uniquely a lie told in soliloquy—but suggests that we can nonetheless see a falling off in the literary genealogy of Autolycus, who in several classical sources is a superior man.

To the first audience Bohemia might well have appeared relatively modern because, aside from the monarchy, there are no visible aristocrats in Bohemia, only self-made men, and none but aristocrats in Sicilia. The health and vitality of Bohemia is in contrast to Sicilia's decay, and it is an injection of what makes Bohemia healthy that brings about the final transformation of Sicilia. Paulina performs a double life-giving ceremony when she appears to transform a statue into living flesh and simultaneously brings Hermione back from the dead. As Anne Barton pointed out, Shakespeare's use of the name of a real-life near-contemporary of the dramatist, Julio Romano, is unique to this work and serves to evoke a 'demonstrable reality' (Barton 1990, 86), a specificity of time and place running against the play's ahistorical elements, the Ceres myth and the universals of human behaviour. The play is firmly located by this casually dropped name, pinned to the Italian Renaissance and the associations that go with it. The most important of these for the contemporary audience would have been the association of Italy with forward-looking ideas in politics and the role of the bourgeoisie. The rise of mercantilism, the erosion of ancient feudal structures, and most especially the geographical and social mobility of the new bourgeoisie underlie this only superficially Mediterranean drama.

In the Shepherd and his son there is another kind of social mobility: lacking Camillo's merit, they rose by the lucky find of Perdita and the wealth that Antigonus left with her. In the Shepherd's instruction to Perdita 'Pray you bid / These unknown friends to 's welcome, for it is / A way to make us better friends, more known' (4.4.64–6) we might hear not only a desire to increase friendship generally but also to acquire friends who are 'better' *because* 'more known'. The rustics' lack of honourable feeling contrasts sharply with Camillo's uprightness, evidenced in their willingness to throw Perdita off to save themselves from Polixenes's wrath:

CLOWN She being none of your flesh and blood, your flesh and blood has not
  offended the King, and so your flesh and blood is not to be punished by him.
  Show those things you found about her, those secret things, all but what she
  has with her. This being done, let the law go whistle, I warrant you.
OLD SHEPHERD I will tell the King all, every word, yea,

(4.4.693–9)

Their shallowness reveals a hollow aspect to social advancement: they move up by taking a member of the aristocracy into their family but ties so easily made are easily broken.

When the Shepherd and his son achieve a permanent elevation at the end of the play, much fun is made of their notions of innate gentility:

AUTOLYCUS I know you are now, sir, a gentleman born.
CLOWN Ay, and have been so any time these four hours.
OLD SHEPHERD And so have I, boy.
CLOWN So you have; but I was a gentleman born before my father, for the
  King's son took me by the hand and called me brother; and then the two
  kings called my father brother; and then the Prince my brother and the
  Princess my sister called my father father; and so we wept; and there was the
  first gentleman-like tears that ever we shed.

(5.2.134–43)

Social mobility is not represented as an unadulterated good. For all its nobility and material plenitude, Bohemia's ruler retains an aristocratic snobbery in violently rejecting low-born (as he thinks) Perdita as his son's chosen wife, and the Shepherd and his son quickly become snobs once elevated.

Only the mobility of the worthy Camillo is approved of by the play, and it is a worth manifested in his having great prospects and jeopardizing them in order not to have to obey the king's command to kill Polixenes. A strict accounting of his own profit is not enough to sway Camillo's principles:

> To do this deed,
> Promotion follows. If I could find example
> Of thousands that had struck anointed kings
> And flourished after, I'd not do 't. But since
> Nor brass, nor stone, nor parchment bears not one,
> Let villainy itself forswear 't.

> (1.2.357–62)

The principle alone is enough to stay his hand, but the pragmatist goes on to square this with a rational evaluation that historical precedent confirms the principle. Camillo's honour is manifested in respect for the traditional view of monarchy and in his putting principle above material gain. In this he is a role model for the new bourgeoisie.

The bourgeoisie were gaining status on the basis of their increasing economic power. Shakespeare engaged in the debate over the propriety of such men having influence at court by presenting them as acceptable so long as honourable, offering a redefinition of worthiness that squared it with the inevitable. The increasing power of the bourgeoisie had to be accepted so the aristocracy reasserted the criterion of chivalric honour (the placing of principles before material considerations) for membership of the ruling class in order to present their privileges as just. Honour so defined might conceivably form the basis of a meritocratic solution to the slowly developing political crises, and its reassertion was driven by erosion of real aristocratic power.

In a study of the steady polarization of monarchy on one side and the gentry and the populace on the other—that is, the declining economic and military power of the aristocracy as an intermediary class—Lawrence Stone traced the so-called 'aristocratic revival' of the late-sixteenth and early-seventeenth centuries:

... the nobility were losing their nerve. As their utility in war declined, they tried to protect their position by a romantic and artificial revival of the chivalric ideal, expressed in literature by Malory's Arthurian legends, by Lord Berners's translation of Froissart, and by Stephen Hawes's *The Pastime of Pleasure*. These calls for a spiritual regeneration in military prowess to justify social and economic privilege were doomed to failure in the face of technical changes in war and the revolution in concepts of duty. (Stone 1965, 266)

The chivalric ideal had at its centre the idea of magnanimity, and this is what the aristocracy wished to present as the difference between themselves and anyone who threatened them. In *The Winter's Tale* we see Shakespeare presenting a solution to class conflict by having the bourgeoisie live up to the rules of honourable behaviour that the aristocracy had devised to justify themselves.

Marx cautioned that in modelling class conflict we must not mistake an abstraction for reality, which is made of particular people engaged in particular activities and not simply fulfilling an assigned historical function. Although the classes were far from homogeneous and the aristocracy played a major part in providing venture-capital for this stage in the capitalist development of England—a point that Shakespeare made central to *The Merchant of Venice*, where we began—there was undoubtedly a class conflict in the making. Its eruption into open warfare in 1642 brought to an end the dramatic tradition that Shakespeare's plays, above all others, helped to define.

Marx and Genetics

As Marx was working on the plan for *Capital* there appeared in London another work on the large-scale effects of competition, Charles Darwin's *The Origin of Species* (1859). Darwin was aware of an important problem with his book: according to the prevailing model of reproduction in which parental characteristics were thought to be blended, small improvements in an individual's suitedness to its environment (the unit of change in his model of natural selection) would be diluted not built upon. Ideas about inheritance were dominated by Chevalier de Lamarck's view that an individual's children inherit characteristics (say, well-developed arm muscles) created by an individual's behaviour (say, working as a blacksmith). Lacking Gregor Mendel's particulate model of heredity, Darwinism could look awkwardly teleological in explaining increased specialization and adaptation as though they were manifestations of creatures' striving towards a goal. Ironically, Lamarckism survived into the second half of the twentieth century via the utterly mistaken ideas of T. D. Lysenko, who controlled, and thus impeded, genetic research in the Soviet Union.

Marx's work was equally susceptible to a charge of teleology, apparently explaining epochal change as progression towards the goal of a workers' paradise. The parallels between Marx and Darwin were clear at the time and indeed it was entirely plausible (although, as it happens, untrue) that Marx offered to dedicate an edition of *Capital* to Darwin, and Engels famously made the connection in his funeral speech for Marx: 'Just as Darwin discovered the law of evolution in organic nature, so Marx discovered the law of evolution in human history' (Margaret 1978; Foner 1973, 39). The rediscovery of Mendel's work by Carl Correns, Erich Tschermak von Seysenegg, and Hugo de Vries in 1900 gave birth to neo-Darwinism, capable of explaining progress without teleology. It is commonly thought that neo-Darwinism posits a gradual and steady change in the genetic codes of organisms and that this contrasts with Marx's segmental model of change in which a system of production remains in place for a whole epoch, only to be rapidly and radically overhauled when excessively out of step with productive forces. The truth is somewhat more complex.

Just as it inherits its language and history from its predecessors, each generation inherits from the past a genetic code that was adapted to the conditions of the past. Being alive proves that, against the odds, each of one's ancestors, stretching back through pre-human history, managed to avoid premature death and reproduced itself. This formidable genetic inheritance—the absence of bad genes that would have killed or made infertile an ancestor—is the consequence of innumerable small changes in the genome, necessarily small because large mutations almost always produce unhealthy individuals who do not survive to adulthood. There tend not to be abrupt changes in evolution: new developments can only grow from what already exists.

Equally, however, the principle of slow change means that we carry genes, and the expressed consequences of those genes, long after the purpose they served—or more precisely, the circumstances that favoured them—have disappeared. We humans have an appendix for processing cellulose although we long since stopped eating it, and as embryos we show gill-like vestiges of an even earlier period of our ancestry. The likeness between this genetic circumstance and Raymond Williams's model of residual cultures (pp. 77–80 above) is instructive since Williams's model was entirely compatible with a Marxist view of rapid epoch-changing upheaval. Generational variations must be understood at the level of the gene itself, which behaves in a way that can be likened to selfishness. That is to say, genes cause the vehicles they inhabit, bodies, to behave in ways that give those genes the best chance of being reproduced. There is no intentionality involved here; it is simply that genes that do otherwise tend to disappear by natural selection because they are competing with other genes that do this.

In his book *The Selfish Gene* (1976) Richard Dawkins showed that a model of competing genes makes sense of animal behaviour that a model of competing individuals cannot explain. It used to be difficult to explain why some creatures appear to behave altruistically to their fellows and others do not, and why some animals fight ferociously to assert their dominance within a group and others give up after a short period of posturing. Thinking in terms of groups trying to do the best for themselves against other groups leads to an even greater muddle and can at worst imply a collective foresight of which animals are incapable. When one considers animals (including people) as machines built by genes for the better success of their own replication, these behaviours become explicable. The particular circumstances experienced by a given population of animals—the scarcity of resources, the danger from predators, and the degrees of consanguinity—will determine whether genes are best to have their phenotypes (the bodies they have built for themselves) co-operate or compete, and the specific ways in which they do these things.

Genes are in competition with other genes, certainly, but related individuals will share some genes, so the environment within which a gene is operating includes copies of itself inside other bodies. Altruism such as alerting one's relatives when one has found food can be the best policy for a selfish gene if the slightly diminished nutritional loss occasioned by sharing the food is offset by a gain to relatives who probably contain copies of the same gene. What appears to be concern for others shown by an individual in the group is actually just an expression of the gene's concern for itself. It is worth stressing again that this is only a metaphor: the genes are not actually selfish, but seem so because genes that behave otherwise tend to lose the competition for replication because the vehicles they build die before reproducing. Genes that promote the ability to make such cost-benefit analyses (including the ability to identify one's relatives) have an evolutionary advantage over ones that do not, and will be naturally selected.

The Shakespeare Meme

In his chapter 'Memes: The New Replicators' (1989, 189–201), Dawkins tentatively explored the possibility that the same phenomena observed in genetic replication occur in human minds too. Ideas are reproduced by spreading from one mind to another, and over time the accumulation of small changes produces great differences:

Geoffrey Chaucer could not hold a conversation with a modern Englishman, even though they are linked to each other by an unbroken chain of some twenty generations of Englishmen, each of whom could speak to his immediate neighbours in the chain as a son speaks to his father. Language seems to 'evolve' by non-genetic means, and at a rate which is orders of magnitude faster than genetic evolution. (Dawkins 1989, 189)

Dawkins coined the word 'meme' to stand for any unit of cultural copying, such as the fashion of wearing a baseball cap back-to-front or believing in God.

Memes spread by being attractive to their hosts, our minds. Belief in an afterlife has benefits of solace in times of trouble and provides a rationale for passive responses to adversity. These benefits align with other human tendencies and so promote this meme's replication through millions of minds. The pattern of neuron connection that constitutes an idea is thus materially replicated as the meme spreads like a virus from one mind to the next, and once the environment (human culture and social intercourse) required for this dissemination came into being it was virtually inevitable that replicating memes would spring into existence.

One class of memes has proved exceedingly well suited to getting itself copied by generations of speakers, first in English and subsequently in all the major world languages: the Shakespeare plays. The primary means of written replication of the Shakespeare canon in its first century was by the reprinting of a recent edition with accumulated editorial changes, rather than by returning to the editions printed in Shakespeare's time, so that an analogy with genetic progression roughly holds for this period (Murphy 2003, pp. 36–79). In Chapter 4 (pp. 116–17 above) we saw the continuance of this into the eighteenth century when William Warburton's emendation added to the error of Alexander Pope's version of the Fool's 'I'll speak a prophecy ere I go' (*King Lear*, 3.2.79–80).

The plays also replicate in performance, of course, and here the analogy holds for much longer because actors often locate their interpretation of a role within a lineage. In his *Roscius Anglicanus* (1708) John Downes attributed the quality of Thomas Betterton's performance in the role of Hamlet to instructions transmitted via William Davenant, who had seen 'Mr. Taylor of the Blackfriars Company' perform it, having been 'instructed by the author Mr. Shakespeare', and likewise Betterton's Henry VIII came from Davenant, 'who had it from old Mr Lowin, that had his instructions from Mr Shakespeare himself' (Salgādo 1975, 61–2). The practice continues: Ian McKellen's film performance as Richard III (Loncraine 1995) is at once in the camp tradition of Laurence Olivier's film (Olivier 1955) that in turn drew on a tradition from Colley Cibber, and defines itself against specific parts of that tradition (Buhler 2000).

In popular culture and language the plays have a greater currency still, a phenomenon traced by Douglas Lanier (2002). Shakespearian quotations in popular usage are often slightly wrong, as with 'Alas poor Yorick, I knew him well' and 'Lead on, Macduff'. Dawkins considered the 'corruption' of singing the words 'For the sake of Auld Lang Syne', a phrase that does not appear in Robert Burns's lyrics of the song and probably crept in by error of aural copying (Dawkins 1989, 323–4). Dawkins concluded that once the error occurred it survived because few people ever see the song written down and the incorrect phrasing is more audible than the correct phrasing (just 'For Auld Lang Syne') when sung together, so that anyone who learns the song by joining in a singing group is likely to pick up the former rather than the latter. The replicability of the incorrect phrasing is stronger than that of the correct phrasing, and by the genetic analogy this is what matters for survival.

Likewise, 'Alas, poor Yorick. I knew him, Horatio' (*Hamlet*, 5.1.180) comes from a dialogue, and taken out of context it is not obvious what the last word is for; the substitution of 'well' renders the quotation a meaningful, self-contained unit that replicates more easily than the original. Similarly, 'Lay on, Macduff' (*Macbeth* 5.10.33) uses the now-unfamiliar intransitive sense of 'lay' meaning attack (*OED* lay $v.^1$ 55b) and is less likely to be copied than 'Lead on, Macduff', which can be used in everyday interaction.

From a memetic perspective, theatres, schools, and universities are the Shakespeare plays' ways of making more copies of themselves. As with the transmission of language in general, those 'infected' with the Shakespeare meme tend to spread it by bringing children to the theatre at an early age, and public examinations exclude those who do not have it, or cannot at least fake the symptoms. Having read or seen Shakespeare, many people are so taken with it that they buy copies of his books and books about him and his works (stimulating the spread of the Shakespeare meme in print), and they go to the theatre and encourage others to do so (spreading the meme in performance). They might also feel this way about Ben Jonson or Christopher Marlowe, but it seems that few people find these strains as infectious as Shakespeare. On this view, the theatre world of Renaissance London was just an ideal environment for hotbedding the hardiest dramatic memes.

The memetic analogy from genes gives anyone working on culture a new way to think about the transmission and longevity of ideas. Determining which features of the capitalist world properly belong in the base and which in the superstructure has long been a problem for Marxists. Clearly, ideas operate in the base as well as the superstructure, so one cannot simply declare that the base is the 'doing' and the superstructure is the 'thinking' that goes along with the doing, rationalizing and validating it. Genetic biologists are apt to see the effects of genes extending as far as the body of the individual that the genes create, and they prefer a different set of terms (behaviour, instinct, and in some cases community) for what the individual then does in the world.

In *The Extended Phenotype* (1982), Dawkins persuasively argued that this distinction is false: webs made to catch prey or dams blocking rivers are as much the results of a spider's or a beaver's genes as are hairy legs or razor-sharp teeth. The limit of the body is a useful one for certain kinds of analysis and practice: if one wants to help a sick beaver one operates on the animal rather than the dam it built. However, for other kinds of analysis and practice the body is not the right subject; to get a healthy population of beavers one needs to ensure the survival of habitats they can dam. This serves as an analogy for the limitations of the base/superstructure model, which likewise has validity in certain contexts but need not be taken as a real distinction. All the thinking that goes along with capitalist production is part of the environment to which that production must be adapted; yet at the same time that environment is shaped by the production.

Marx and Darwin felt their works' affinity at the time, but their intellectual inheritors could scarcely be more antagonistic. In truth the fault lies mostly with the Marxists. The constructivist model of language and culture (pp. 18–22 above) has long dominated the literary end of the social sciences, an enduring legacy of Saussure despite the linguists abandoning him 50 year ago. Saussure had little to say about language acquisition, but the influential applications of his ideas by the anthropologist Claude Lévi-Strauss, the psychoanalyst Jacques Lacan, and the philosopher Jacques Derrida have tended to see the system (Saussure's *langue*) as essentially embodied in social practice. We are born into a world of existing language (in its widest sense including myths, rituals, and other cultural practices) and acquire our identities by learning to adapt to it.

Noam Chomsky, however, argued that this was simply impossible: language is learnt too quickly, and with too few negative stimuli—lessons drawn from our mistakes in forming sentences—for the empiricist model to be correct. Instead, some of the core principles of language use must be innate (Chomsky 1965, 47–58). For structuralists, meaning is in the relationships between elements in a system, so there are no positive terms only webs of difference, and as we have seen this idea had immense philosophical attraction for a wide range of theorists in the social sciences. By positing an innate language faculty inside the evolved human mind, Chomsky changed the terms of the debate from an analysis of something 'out there' in cultural practice to something that psychologists and biologists might throw light upon. Such hard science has long been the terror of left-wing cultural theory.

Uncomfortable as it is, the innateness of things that we previously thought were cultural has become irrefutable. Emotions expressed facially in one culture have turned out to be readily understood in entirely different cultures (Ekman, Friesen, and Ellsworth 1972, 153–67). Of course culture modifies these behaviours, as when poker players train themselves not to show emotion facially, but it does not construct them. The same is true regarding differentiation of colour, which is relatively invariant across cultures and determined by innate brain function not social practice (Berlin and Kay 1969).

It might seem that we have here an inside-the-mind camp of theorists beginning to defeat an outside-the-mind camp, but such a distinction is unhelpful. Just as a beaver's dam or a spider's web should really be considered as phenotypic effects of beaver and spider genes, so libraries and churches should be considered effects of the language and religion memes; drawing the line at the individual human mind is as artificial as drawing the line at the individual beaver body. Lévi-Strauss had already stated a meme-eye view of the world of myths in much the way that Dawkins later stated the gene-eye and meme-eye views, in his 'I thus do not aim to show how men think in myths but how myths think in men, unbeknownst to them' (Lévi-Strauss 1970, 20).

Stability and Historical Change

It is a principle of evolution that only small changes can happen between generations; large changes are likely to produce new infants not viable under the current conditions. This does not mean, however, that societies can only change by increments. Dawkins explored a number of population systems that achieve a stable equilibrium only to flip to a new equilibrium under the right conditions. Dawkins's prime example was a modelling of the so-called 'Prisoner's Dilemma' scenario that in David Edgar's play, with which I began Chapter 1, is likened also to the negotiations that take place between terrorists and governments in newly emerging states (Dawkins 1989, 202–33).

The scenario concerns two prisoners suspected of a serious crime and interrogated independently. Each may confess or remain silent but knows that if both of them are silent the main charges will be dropped for lack of evidence (although they will both get short sentences for related minor offences), and if both confess they will both get a moderate prison term. However, if one confesses while the other remains silent, the confessor will go free and the silent one will get a long prison term. One can also think of this scenario as a game in which each of two participants chooses to either 'co-operate with' or 'defect upon' the other, there being a small bonus for mutual co-operation, a penalty for mutual defection, and a large bonus for being the one who defects when the other, a 'sucker', co-operates.

Without knowing how the other will act, a player must consider her best policy given two possible actions by the opponent, who will either co-operate or will defect. Taking each of the two possibilities in turn, a sensible prisoner will reason as follows. 'Suppose I knew that the other person has decided to co-operate, what would my best course of action be? To defect, obviously, making a "sucker" of her and collecting the large bonus for doing so. Now, suppose instead that the other person is going to defect, what were my best course? Why, again it is to defect in order to prevent her making a "sucker" of me. So, no matter what the other person does, my best course of action is to defect.' Since both players will reason this way it is inevitable that both will defect. If only the players/prisoners could conspire they were best to agree to co-operate, but denied conference they must, each acting in her own interests, defect.

Although the rules do not allow conspiring, the game can be repeated many times to give each player a 'history', a track record, of the other's behaviour upon which to base decisions. If one's opponent is an unshakeable co-operator, one were best to defect every time and so claim the large bonuses for making a 'sucker' of her. However, if one's opponent were consistently playing the same policy, and also learning from 'history', this aggressive policy would be self-defeating. Dawkins described an experiment by Robert M. Axelrod, who asked for interested parties to contribute strategies for a computer model of a Prisoner's Dilemma tournament, each strategy having to play a fixed number of rounds against each of the others and against a copy of itself.

Many complex and fiendish strategies were submitted, but the tournament was won by a strategy of beautiful simplicy called Tit for Tat: play 'co-operate' in the first hand and thereafter do whatever the opponent did in the previous round. When a copy of Tit for Tat plays another copy of Tit for Tat, both consistently co-operate (the opening accord is never broken) and reap the bonuses for doing so. When Tit for Tat meets strategies trying to 'sucker' it, it copies them and visits the same on its opponent, but if the opponent mends its ways Tit for Tat ceases the punishment.

In nature the reward for a successful strategy is self-replication: those that do less well in the 'game' of survival are removed from future 'games' because the winners reproduce more quickly. Axelrod incorporated this refinement into a subsequent tournament by rewarding the highest scoring strategies with extra copies of themselves and killing off the lowest scoring strategies. The population of strategies would thus change over time by natural selection. Axelrod found that in his modelling of this part of the phenomenon of natural selection—the numerical dominance of the successful—strategies that tried to co-operate but reciprocated defection, such as Tit for Tat, came to dominate the population. Moreover, the population of strategies settled down to an equilibrium so that after 1,000 iterations of the game, the relative sub-populations of the various strategies ceased to change between iterations.

Depending on the starting ratio of 'nice' (optimistic and forgiving) to 'nasty' (exploitative) strategies, the population after many iterations would settle down to one of two states of equilibrium, the first full of virtuous circles of mutual collaboration and the second full of vicious circles of incessant defection. The second, vicious, system was stable but could be undermined, flipped into the virtuous system with the right kind of intervention while the reverse, a flip from virtuous to vicious, was harder to achieve. The reason for this one-way directionality is local clustering.

In a world dominated by vice, virtuous strategies, although not present in large enough numbers to find each other everywhere, can achieve a mutually beneficial effect from clumping (which can occur by random distribution) so that these local communities behave like miniature versions of the larger population, with all the benefits of local ubiquity. By contrast, vicious strategies do not benefit from clustering; indeed they do better when surrounded by their opposite, virtue. A 'world' dominated by vicious strategies can be made to tip more easily towards virtue than a world of virtuous strategies can be made to tip into vice, even though systems of vice and of virtue might each be stable once achieved.

As we saw with *Timon of Athens* (pp. 106–15 above), individual reciprocity, whether altruistic or selfish, can be extrapolated to larger social circulations of mutually beneficial or mutually destructive behaviour. Shakespeare explored the paradoxical similarities between extreme altruism and extreme malice captured in the closing image of two leeches sucking one another's blood and, read optimistically, the play suggests that vicious circles can be turned into virtuous ones. It would be naive to draw from Axelrod's experiment a simple moral such as 'virtue is stronger than vice', although instructively it undermines the platitude commonly used to defend capitalism that self-interest writ large necessarily produces exploitative relations in a population. However, the results have a greater significance for our understanding of Marx's claim that a fully ripe capitalist system can be flipped over into communism without the upheaval that occurred when feudalism was replaced by capitalism.

The principle of local clustering appears to validate the 'small is beautiful' political activism (such as communes) of the post-1968 disillusionment (pp. 75–7 above): instead of trying to change the entire system one should, by this logic, work to create local systems of mutual co-operation. Marx opposed the idea that local solutions might lead the way from capitalism to communism. Local communism in one place would undoubtedly be destroyed as the capitalist system expanded into every corner of the world. What was needed was an 'all at once' and universal transformation of the world (Marx and Engels 1974, 56).

Axelrod's Prisoner's Dilemma differed from real-world economics in that each strategy played one opponent at a time, whereas in reality a small number of capitalists are 'playing' against a huge number of workers simultaneously. As Marx observed, the workers are already co-operating with each other on an enormous scale, since one group cannot make motor cars unless another is making ball-bearings and another making glass. A single capitalist effectively suckers them all at a stroke. The parallels between real economic interaction and an extremely simple computer model should not be pushed too far, but nor should they be rejected entirely. The principle that complex interactions lead to equilibrium and that more than one equilibrium might be viable is useful, and even more striking is the conclusion that the transition from one equilibrium to another might have a gradient. Although states A and B are fairly stable, the transition from A to B may be much more likely than the transition from B to A, and this we may reasonably call progress if we think state B is better than state A, as may be the case if we value the spread of mutual co-operation.

There is nothing teleological about this progressive directionality. Conceivably, the entire capitalist world could revert to feudalism but there is a systemic pressure in the opposite direction, towards something better than capitalism. For Marx this was communism. As he argued, and as twentieth-century history appears to validate, one should not expect a flip from feudalism straight to communism; one may achieve the likeness of such a flip by massive intervention but the resulting system is likely to flip back to its 'real' stage of development, rapacious early capitalism. As a model of the Bolshevik uprising of 1917 and its consequences, including the present parlous state of the former Soviet Union, such an understanding of stable systems is perfectly apt.

Shakespeare's plays are much concerned with epochal change and the way that individual actions bear upon, and are shaped by, larger historical forces. An analysis of *King Lear* that is concerned only with the king's character cannot account for the sense of historical dislocation that we feel in being brought to ancient Britain only to find characters anticipating futures radically unlike their own present. Equally, to explain Leontes's apparently motiveless jealousy in terms of his relationships with Polixenes and Hermione is not to exhaust *The Winter's Tale*'s meanings, for the personal must be contextualized within mythical (essentially cyclical) and historical (linear) explanations of change that the play alludes to.

Like Marx, Shakespeare's understanding of humanity was unremittingly social and both showed that the fullest expression of individuality is only possible through our relations with other people. In *The Comedy of Errors* the final rejection of hierarchy is made in the name of sociable reciprocity and, in contrast to the doubleness implied by the war and the bed-trick in *All's Well That Ends Well*, the Dromios do not collapse equality into sameness; they retain what D. H. Lawrence called 'the strange reality of Otherness' that emerges when we recognize another as equal but different. This sense of sociability artistically conveyed in Shakespeare was given a firm logical and historical foundation by Marx and, far from being outmoded, it is confirmed by recent work in cybernetics, biology, and philosophy. Representing two ways of expressing essentially the same phenomenon, we can read Shakespeare via Marx and Marx via Shakespeare with an optimistic eye to the future not the past.

Aldous Huxley carried a volume of *Encyclopaedia Britannica* with him wherever he travelled, so that at any one time he had a compendious knowledge of topics united by nothing but their initial letter. The whole encyclopaedia now comes on one low-cost computer disk, and most of the political, economic, and philosophical ideas touched upon in this book can be explored further in its essays and suggested readings. The extraordinary resources of the Marxists Internet Archive are freely available at http://www.marxists.org and can also be had on a computer disk distributed at low cost to those in the wealthy nations and free to everyone else. The archive includes all the major works of Marx and selections from 300 other authors including many of the theorists whose work is discussed here, such as Theodor Adorno, Georg Lukács, and Antonio Gramsci. The only demerit of the archive is the lack of a uniform means of citation by which one might refer readers to its individual contents.

Just as the Oxford Shakespeare gives the general reader virtually all the Shakespeare she needs, almost everything one could want of Marx can be had in print via Eugene Kamenka's splendidly chosen and accurately titled collection *The Portable Karl Marx* (Marx 1983). There is no readily available standard edition of the complete works of Marx, and readers wanting to go beyond Kamenka's selections should consult the individual volumes published by Lawrence and Wishart listed in Works Cited (pp. 153–62 below). Like many books that use this subtitle, Terry Eagleton's *Ideology: An Introduction* (Eagleton 1991) goes into considerable detail about its topic, but its author's incorrigible wit makes the material pleasurably digestible and his skills of intellectual synthesis are unique. Most of Bertolt Brecht's reflections on the relationship between theatre and politics can be found in *Brecht on Theatre* (Brecht 1964). George Bernard Shaw's writings on the same topic are rather more widely distributed and a good starting place is *Shaw on Theatre* (Shaw 1958); from there the reader could proceed to the prefaces to particular plays as listed in Works Cited (p. 160 below).

Louis Althusser's influential essay 'Ideology and Ideological State Apparatuses' (Althusser 1971, 127–86) should be read after Jacques Lacan's 'The Mirror Stage as Formative of the Function of the I as Revealed in Psychoanalytic Experience' upon which it draws (Lacan 1977, 1–7). Both are concisely summarized and then tested to destruction in Eagleton's introduction to ideology. Ferdinand de Saussure did not publish his ideas about the sign, signifier, and signified that have become so deeply embedded in literary studies, and the standard work (in French, 1916) was put together by his students from their lecture notes (Saussure 1960). The great theoretical shift in linguistics that literary studies appear to have almost entirely overlooked began with the difficult work *Syntactic Structures* (Chomsky 1957), and the general reader is warned that the subject has got still more difficult since then.

To explore where New Historicism and Cultural Materialism came from, three of Raymond Williams's books are invaluable: *Culture and Society* (1958), *The Country and the City* (1973), and *Marxism and Literature* (1977). A cogent, but in my view mistaken, argument that apparently Marxist approaches to literature have become indelibly tainted by faulty poststructuralism is the nub of Leonard Jackson's *The Dematerialization of Karl Marx* (Jackson 1994), which is engagingly written and ranges across a wide spectrum of literature. Anyone who is convinced that all is well with literary theory will find in Jackson many objections to it that cannot easily be overcome. One exception, however, is Jackson's repetition of the frequently heard rejection of the Labour Theory of Value in favour of the principle of Marginal Utility. For a fully theorized defence of the Labour Theory of Value by an academic economist, John Weeks's *Capital and Exploitation* (Weeks 1981) is recommended.

A search for 'Marx' and 'Shakespeare' in any good library catalogue returns the recent book *Marxist Shakespeares* (Howard and Shershow 2001), a most uneven collection of essays on the topic. My long review of this is freely available from the Web-delivered journal *Early Modern Literary Studies* (Egan 2001b), but put briefly the essays by Richard Halpern, Natasha Korda, Walter Cohen, Richard Wilson, Kiernan Ryan, and most especially Scott Cutler Shershow (to which I refer several times above) are clearly written and proceed by logical progression from theoretical premises and textual evidence to meaningful conclusions. The remainder do not, because either the theory is so dense as to be unintelligible even to the sympathetic reader or the evidence is overstretched or ignored; frequently both faults arise.

Finally, for an argument that Marxist political and cultural theory can, indeed must, incorporate the latest development in street politics—by which I mean the broad coalition of eco-warriors, anarchists, animal rights protesters, and anti-capitalists that has become visible in the past few years—I shamelessly recommend my next book, *Green Shakespeare: from Ecopolitics to Ecocriticism* (Egan 2005). Deriving directly from the ecological movements of the 1980s and 1990s, ecocriticism reinforces the link between politics and literature evident in English studies' continuing commitment to feminist, postcolonial, and queer studies. Ecocritical debates concur in a passionate rejection of key aspects of late-industrial capitalism such as globalization, the manipulation of genetic data, and the exploitation of animals. This book traces the origins of ecocriticism in ecological writing and science and argues for the special contribution this kind of criticism can make to our understanding of Shakespeare.

Works Cited

Abraham, Lyndy (1998). *A Dictionary of Alchemical Imagery*. Cambridge: Cambridge University Press.

Adorno, Theodor (1973). *Negative Dialectics*, trans. E. B. Ashton. London: Routledge.

Althusser, Louis (1971). *Lenin and Philosophy and Other Essays*, trans. Ben Brewster. London: Monthly Review Press.

Bamber, Linda (1982). *Comic Women, Tragic Men: A Study of Gender and Genre in Shakespeare*. Stanford, Calif.: Stanford University Press.

Barton, Anne (1990). *The Names of Comedy*. Oxford: Clarendon.

Bate, Jonathan (2000). 'Shakespeare's Foolosophy', *Shakespeare Performed: Essays in Honor of R. A. Foakes*, ed. Grace Ioppolo. Newark, N. J.: University of Delaware Press, 17–32.

Baudrillard, Jean (1995). *The Gulf War Did Not Take Place*, trans. Paul Patton. Bloomington, Ind.: Indiana University Press.

Belsey, Catherine (1985a). 'Disrupting Sexual Difference: Meaning and Gender in the Comedies', *Alternative Shakespeares*, ed. John Drakakis. London: Routledge, 166–90.

——(1985b). *The Subject of Tragedy: Identity and Difference in Renaissance Drama*. London, Methuen.

——(1991). 'Afterword: A Future for Materialist Feminist Criticism?', *The Matter of Difference: Materialist Feminist Criticism of Shakespeare*, ed. Valerie Wayne. Ithaca, N.Y.: Cornell University Press, 257–70.

Berger, Peter L., and Luckman, Thomas (1967). *The Social Construction of Reality*. Harmondsworth: Penguin.

Berlin, Brent, and Kay, Paul (1969). *Basic Color Terms: Their Universality and Evolution*. Berkeley, Calif.: University of California Press.

Berry, Ralph (1981). *Shakespearean Structures*. Basingstoke: Macmillan.

Bowers, Fredson (1980). 'Shakespeare at Work: The Foul Papers of *All's Well That Ends Well*', *English Renaissance Studies Presented to Dame Helen Gardner in Honour of Her Seventieth Birthday*, ed. John Carey. Oxford: Oxford University Press, 56–73.

Bradshaw, Graham (1993). *Misrepresentations: Shakespeare and the Materialists*. Ithaca, N.Y.: Cornell University Press.

——(2001). 'The "Encrusted" *Hamlet*: Resetting the "Mousetrap"', *Approaches to Teaching Shakespeare's Hamlet*, ed. Bernice W. Kliman.

Approaches to Teaching World Literature. New York: Modern Language Association of America, 118–28.

Bray, Alan (1982). *Homosexuality in Renaissance England*. London: Gay Men's Press.

Brecht, Bertolt (1964). *Brecht on Theatre*, ed. and trans. John Willett. London: Methuen.

——(1965). *The Messingkauf Dialogues*. London: Methuen.

Buhler, Stephen M. (2000). 'Camp *Richard III* and the Burdens of (Stage/film) History', *Shakespeare, Film, Fin de Siècle*, ed. Mark Thornton Burnett and Ramona Wray. Basingstoke: Macmillan, 40–57.

Bullough, Geoffrey (1958). *Narrative and Dramatic Sources of Shakespeare. Vol. 2: The Comedies, 1597–1603 [The Merry Wives of Windsor; Much Ado About Nothing; As You Like It; Twelfth Night; All's Well That Ends Well; Measure for Measure]*. London: Routledge and Kegan Paul.

——(1973). *Narrative and Dramatic Sources of Shakespeare. Vol. 7: Major Tragedies: [Hamlet; Othello; King Lear; Macbeth]*. London: Routledge and Kegan Paul.

Cady, Joseph (1992). ' "Masculine Love", Renaissance Writing, and the "New Invention" of Homosexuality', *Homosexuality in Renaissance and Enlightenment England: Literary Representations in Historical Context*, ed. Claude J. Summers. New York: Haworth Press, 9–40.

Calderwood, James L. (1971). *Shakespearean Metadrama: The Argument of the Play in* Titus Andronicus, Love's Labour's Lost, Romeo and Juliet, A Midsummer Night's Dream, *and* Richard II. Minneapolis, Minn.: University of Minnesota Press.

Campbell, Lily B. (1947). *Shakespeare's 'Histories': Mirrors of Elizabethan Policy*. San Marino, Calif.: Huntington Library.

Caudwell, Christopher (1937). *Illusion and Reality: A Study of the Sources of Poetry*. London: Macmillan.

——(1938). *Studies in a Dying Culture*. London: John Lane.

——(1939). *The Crisis in Physics*, ed. and introd. Hyman Levy. London: John Lane.

Chambers, E. K. (1923). *The Elizabethan Stage*. Vol. 4. Oxford: Clarendon Press.

Chomsky, Noam (1957). *Syntactic Structures*. Janua Linguarum Series Minor. 4. The Hague: Mouton.

——(1965). *Aspects of the Theory of Syntax*. Cambridge, Mass.: Massachusetts Institute of Technology University Press.

Dawkins, Richard (1976). *The Selfish Gene*. Oxford: Oxford University Press.

Dawkins, Richard (1982). *The Extended Phenotype: The Gene as the Unit of Selection*. Oxford: Oxford University Press.

—— (1989). *The Selfish Gene*, second edn. Oxford: Oxford University Press.

De Beauvoir, Simone (1953). *The Second Sex*, ed. H. M. Parshley. London: Jonathan Cape.

Dent, R. W. (1981). *Shakespeare's Proverbial Language: An Index*. Berkeley, Calif.: University of California Press.

Derrida, Jacques (1976). *Of Grammatology*, trans. Gayatri Chakrovorty Spivak. Baltimore, Md.: Johns Hopkins University Press.

—— (1994). *Specters of Marx: The State of the Debt, the Work of Mourning, and the New International*, trans. Peggy Kamuf. London: Routledge.

Dollimore, Jonathan (1984). *Radical Tragedy: Religion, Ideology and Power in the Drama of Shakespeare and His Contemporaries*. Hemel Hempstead: Harvester Wheatsheaf.

—— (1989). *Radical Tragedy: Religion, Ideology and Power in the Drama of Shakespeare and His Contemporaries*, second edn. Hemel Hempstead: Harvester Wheatsheaf.

—— and Sinfield, Alan (1985a). 'Foreword: Cultural Materialism', *Political Shakespeare: New Essays in Cultural Materialism*, ed. Jonathan Dollimore and Alan Sinfield. Manchester: Manchester University Press, vii–viii.

—— and Sinfield, Alan (eds.) (1985b). *Political Shakespeare: New Essays in Cultural Materialism*. Manchester: Manchester University Press.

Downes, John (1708). *Roscius Anglicanus, or an Historical Review of the Stage*. London: H. Playford.

Drakakis, John (ed.) (1985). *Alternative Shakespeares*. London: Routledge.

Dusinberre, Juliet (1975). *Shakespeare and the Nature of Women*. New York: Barnes and Noble.

Eagleton, Terry (1991). *Ideology: An Introduction*. London: Verso.

—— (2001). *The Gatekeeper: A Memoir*. London: Penguin.

Eco, Umberto (1977). 'Semiotics of Theatrical Performance'. *The Drama Review* 21: 107–17.

Edgar, David (2001). *The Prisoner's Dilemma*. London: Nick Hern Books.

Egan, Gabriel (2001a). 'Hearing or Seeing a Play?: Evidence of Early Modern Theatrical Terminology'. *Ben Jonson Journal*. 8: 327–47.

—— (2001b). 'Review of Jean E. Howard and Scott Cutler Shershow *Marxist Shakespeares* (London: Routledge, 2001)'. *Early Modern Literary Studies* 7.2. Available at http://www.shu.ac.uk/emls/07-2/eganrev.html

—— (2005). *Green Shakespeare: from Ecopolitics to Ecocriticism*. New Accents on Shakespeare. London: Routledge.

Ekman, Paul, Friesen, Wallace V., and Ellsworth, Phoebe (1972). *Emotion in the Human Face: Guidelines for Research and an Integration of Findings.* Pergamon General Psychology Series. 11. New York: Pergamon.

Empson, William (1951). *The Structure of Complex Words.* London: Chatto and Windus.

Fay, Margaret A. (1978). 'Did Marx Offer to Dedicate *Capital* to Darwin?: A Reassessment of the Evidence'. *Journal of the History of Ideas* 39: 133–46.

Foner, Philip (ed.) (1973). *When Karl Marx Died: Comments in 1883.* New York: International Publishers.

Fox, Ralph (1937). *The Novel and the People.* London: Lawrence and Wishart.

Gramsci, Antonio (1971). *Selections from the Prison Notebooks*, ed. and trans. Quintin Hoare and Geoffrey Nowell Smith. London: Lawrence and Wishart.

Gray, J. C. (1986). 'Shakespeare and the New Oxford English Dictionary'. *Shakespeare Bulletin* 4: 5–7.

Greenblatt, Stephen (1980). *Renaissance Self-fashioning: From More to Shakespeare.* Chicago: University of Chicago Press.

—— (1985). 'Invisible Bullets: Renaissance Authority and Its Subversion, *Henry IV* and *Henry V* ', *Political Shakespeare: New Essays in Cultural Materialism*, ed. Jonathan Dollimore and Alan Sinfield. Manchester: Manchester University Press, 18–47.

—— (1988). *Shakespearean Negotiations: The Circulation of Social Energy in Renaissance England.* Oxford: Clarendon Press.

—— (1990). *Learning to Curse: Essays in Early Modern Culture.* New York: Routledge.

Greg, W. W. (1917). 'Hamlet's Hallucination'. *Modern Language Review* 12: 393–421.

Gurr, Andrew (2002). 'Headgear as Paralinguistic Signifier in *King Lear*'. *Shakespeare Survey* 55: 43–52.

Hawkes, Terence (1986). *That Shakespeherian Rag: Essays on a Critical Process.* London: Methuen.

—— (1992). *Meaning By Shakespeare.* London: Routledge.

—— (2002). *Shakespeare in the Present.* Accents on Shakespeare. London: Routledge.

Holland, Peter (1991). 'Evading *King Lear*'. *Poetica* 33: 48–62.

—— (2001). '*The Merchant of Venice* and the Value of Money'. *Cahiers Élisabéthains* 60: 13–30.

Holquist, Michael (1990). *Dialogism: Bakhtin and His World.* New Accents. London: Routledge.

Hopkins, Lisa (2000). '"Base Foot-ball Player": The Sporting Life in *King Lear*'. *English Language Notes* 37(4): 8–19.

Howard, Jean E., and Shershow, Scott Cutler (eds.) (2001). *Marxist Shakespeares*. Accents on Shakespeare. London: Routledge.

Hunt, Alan (1996). *Governance of the Consuming Passions: A History of Sumptuary Law*. Basingstoke: Macmillan.

Jackson, Leonard (1994). *The Dematerialisation of Karl Marx: Literature and Marxist Theory*. Foundations of Modern Literary Theory. London: Longman.

Johnson, Samuel (ed.) (1773). *A Dictionary of the English Language*, 4th edn. Vol. 1: A to Kyd. London: W. Strahan.

Jones, Emrys (1971). *Scenic Form in Shakespeare*. Oxford: Clarendon Press.

Kantorowicz, Ernst H. (1957). *The King's Two Bodies: A Study in Mediaeval Political Theology*. Princeton, N.J.: Princeton University Press.

Kavanagh, James (1985). 'Shakespeare in Ideology'. *Alternative Shakespeares*, ed. John Drakakis. New Accents. London: Routledge, 144–65.

Kelly, Henry Ansgar (1970). *Divine Providence in the England of Shakespeare's Histories*. Cambridge, Mass.: Harvard University Press.

Kerrigan, John (1983). 'Revision, Adaptation, and the Fool in *King Lear*', *The Division of the Kingdoms: Shakespeare's Two Versions of* King Lear, ed. Gary Taylor and Michael Warren. Oxford Shakespeare Studies. Oxford: Oxford University Press, 195–243.

Knowles, Richard (2002). 'How Shakespeare Knew *King Leir*'. *Shakespeare Survey* 55: 12–35.

Lacan, Jacques (1977). *Écrits: A Selection*, trans. Alan Sheridan. London: Tavistock.

Lanier, Douglas (2002). *Shakespeare and Modern Popular Culture*. Oxford Shakespeare Topics. Oxford: Oxford University Press.

Lenz, Carolyn Ruth Swift, Greene, Gayle, and Neely, Carol Thomas (1980a). 'Introduction', *The Woman's Part: Feminist Criticism of Shakespeare*, ed. Carolyn Ruth Swift Lenz, Gayle Greene, and Carol Thomas Neely. Urbana, Ill.: University of Illinois Press, 3–16.

——, —— and —— (1980b). *The Woman's Part: Feminist Criticism of Shakespeare*. Urbana, Ill.: University of Illinois Press.

Levin, Richard (1980). 'The Relation of External Evidence to the Allegorical and Thematic Interpretation of Shakespeare'. *Shakespeare Studies* 13: 1–29.

Levine, Laura (1986). 'Men in Women's Clothing: Anti-theatricality and Effeminization from 1579 to 1642'. *Criticism* 28: 121–43.

—— (1994). *Men in Women's Clothing: Anti-theatricality and Effeminization, 1579–1642*. Cambridge Studies in Renaissance Literature and Culture. 5. Cambridge: Cambridge University Press.

Lévi-Strauss, Claude (1968). *The Elementary Structures of Kinship*, trans. James Harle Bell, John Richard von Sturmer, and Rodney Needham. London: Eyre and Spottiswoode.

Lévi-Strauss, Claude (1970). *The Raw and the Cooked*, trans. John and Doreen Weightman. Mythologiques: Introduction to the Science of Mythology. 1. London: Cape.

——(1973). *From Honey to Ashes*, trans. John and Doreen Weightman. Mythologiques: Introduction to the Science of Mythology. 2. London: Cape.

——(1978). *The Origin of Table Manners*, trans. John and Doreen Weightman. Mythologiques: Introduction to the Science of Mythology. 3. London: Cape.

——(1981). *The Naked Man*, trans. John and Doreen Weightman. Mythologiques: Introduction to the Science of Mythology. 4. London: Cape.

Loncraine, Richard (1995). *Richard III*. Motion Picture. Bayly/Pare/United Artists.

Lukács, Georg (1971). *History and Class Consciousness: Studies in Marxist Dialectics*, trans. Rodney Livingstone. London: Merlin Press.

Lyotard, Jean-François (1984). *The Postmodern Condition: A Report on Knowledge*, trans. Geoff Bennington and Brian Massumi. Theory and History of Literature. 10. Manchester: Manchester University Press.

Marcuse, Herbert (1964). *One Dimensional Man: Studies in the Ideology of Advanced Industrial Society*. London: Routledge and Kegan Paul.

Margolies, David (1992). *Monsters of the Deep: Social Dissolution in Shakespeare's Tragedies*. Manchester: Manchester University Press.

Marinetti, Filippo Tommaso (1913). 'Destruction of Syntax—Imagination without Strings—Words-in-freedom.' *Lacerba (Florence)* 15 June. n.p.

Marx, Karl (1899). *Value, Price and Profit: Addressed to Working Men*, ed. Eleanor Marx Aveling. London: George Allen and Unwin.

——(1926). *The Eighteenth Brumaire of Louis Bonaparte*, trans. Eden and Cedar Paul. London: George Allen and Unwin.

——(1954). *Capital: A Critical Analysis of Capitalist Production*, ed. Frederick Engels. Vol. 1. London: Lawrence and Wishart.

——(1970). *A Contribution to the Critique of Political Economy*, ed. and trans. Maurice Dobbs. New York: International Publishers.

——(1977). *Economic and Philosophical Manuscripts of 1844*. London: Lawrence and Wishart.

——(1983). *The Portable Karl Marx*, ed. Eugene Kamenka. New York: Penguin.

——[1935]. *The Poverty of Philosophy*, ed. C. P. Dutt and V. Chattopadhyaya. Introd. Frederick Engels. London: Martin Lawrence.

Marx, Karl, and Engels, Frederick (1948). *The Communist Manifesto*, trans. Samuel Moore (1888): Centenary edn. London: Lawrence and Wishart.

—— and —— (1974). *The German Ideology*, ed. C. J. Arthur. London: Lawrence and Wishart.

McLuskie, Kathleen (1985). 'The Patriarchal Bard: Feminist Criticism and Shakespeare: *King Lear* and *Measure for Measure*', *Political Shakespeare: New Essays in Cultural Materialism*, ed. Jonathan Dollimore and Alan Sinfield. Manchester: Manchester University Press, 88–108.

Monk, Thelonious (1972). *Something in Blue*. Vinyl audio-recording. Sleeve notes by Brian Priestley. Black Lion BL-152/Jazz Man JAZ5019/Polydor 2460.

Murphy, Andrew (2003). *Shakespeare in Print: A History and Chronology of Shakespeare Publishing*. Cambridge. Cambridge University Press.

Norris, Christopher (1985). 'Post-structuralist Shakespeare: Text and Ideology', *Alternative Shakespeares*, ed. John Drakakis. London: Routledge, 47–66.

Olivier, Laurence (1955). *Richard III*. Motion Picture. London Films.

Pitcher, John (2003). 'Some Call Him Autolycus', *In Arden: Editing Shakespeare: Essays in Honour of Richard Proudfoot*, ed. Ann Thompson and Gordon McMullan. The Arden Shakespeare. London: Thomson Learning, 252–68.

Propp, Vladimir (1968). *Morphology of the Folktale*, trans. Laurence Scott, second edn. rev. and ed. Louis A. Wagner. Austin, Tex.: University of Texas Press.

Salgādo, Gāmini (ed.) (1975). *Eyewitnesses of Shakespeare: First Hand Accounts of Performances 1590–1890*. Brighton: Sussex University Press.

Saussure, Ferdinand de (1960). *Course in General Linguistics*, ed. Charles Bally, Albert Sechehaye, and Albert Reidlinger, trans. Wade Baskin. London: Peter Owen.

Scott, Tony (1993). *True Romance*. Motion Picture. August Entertainment/Davis-Films/Morgan Creek.

Shakespeare, William (1747a). *The Works of Shakespear*, ed. William Warburton. *Vol. 6:* King Lear; Timon of Athens; Titus Andronicus; Macbeth; Coriolanus. London: J. and P. Knapton and S. Birt.

—— (1747b). *The Works of Shakespear*, ed. William Warburton. *Vol. 8:* Romeo and Juliet; Hamlet; Othello. London: J. and P. Knapton and S. Birt.

—— (1765a). *The Plays*, ed. Samuel Johnson. *Vol. 1: Preliminary Matter;* The Tempest; A Midsummer-Night's Dream; The Two Gentlemen of Verona; Measure for Measure; The Merchant of Venice. London: J. and R. Tonson [etc.].

—— (1765b). *The Plays*, ed. Samuel Johnson. *Vol. 8:* Romeo and Juliet; Hamlet, Prince of Denmark; Othello, the Moor of Venice; Appendix: Notes on Volumes 1–8. London: J. and R. Tonson [etc.].

Shakespeare, William (1952). *King Lear*, ed. Kenneth Muir. The Arden Shake-speare. London: Methuen.

——(1959). *Timon of Athens*, ed. H. J. Oliver. The Arden Shakespeare. London: Methuen.

——(1960). *King Lear*, ed. George Ian Duthie and John Dover Wilson. The New Shakespeare. Cambridge: Cambridge University Press.

——(1986). *The Complete Works*, ed. Stanley Wells, Gary Taylor, John Jowett, and William Montgomery. Oxford: Oxford University Press.

——(1995). *Titus Andronicus*, ed. Jonathan Bate. Arden Third Series. London: Routledge.

——(1997). *The Norton Shakespeare Based on the Oxford Edition*, ed. Stephen Greenblatt. New York: Norton.

——(2000). *King Lear*, ed. Stanley Wells. The Oxford Shakespeare. Oxford: Oxford University Press.

——(2004). *Timon of Athens*, ed. John Jowett. The Oxford Shakespeare. Oxford: Oxford University Press.

Shaw, George Bernard (1928). *The Intelligent Woman's Guide to Socialism and Capitalism*. London: Constable.

——(1932a). *Our Theatres in the Nineties*. Vol. 2: 4 January 1896–26 December 1896. London: Constable.

——(1932b). *Our Theatres in the Nineties*. Vol. 3: 2 January 1897–21 May 1898. London: Constable.

——(1958). *Shaw on Theatre*. New York: Hill and Wang.

——(1971). *Collected Plays with Their Prefaces*, ed. Dan H. Laurence. *Vol. 2: Three Plays for Puritans* (The Devil's Disciple; Caesar and Cleopatra; Captain Brassbound's Conversion); The Admirable Bashville; Man and Superman; John Bull's Other Island; How He Lied to Her Husband. London: Bodley Head.

——(1972). *Collected Plays with Their Prefaces*, ed. Dan H. Laurence. *Vol. 4*: Misalliance; The Dark Lady of the Sonnets; Fanny's First Play; Androcles and the Lion; Pygmalion; Overruled; The Music-Cure; Great Catherine; The Inca of Perusalem; O'Flaherty, V.C. London: Bodley Head.

——(1974). *Collected Plays with Their Prefaces*, ed. Dan H. Laurence. *Vol. 7*: Geneva; Cymbeline Refinished; 'In Good King Charles's Golden Days'; Buoyant Billions; Farfetched Fables; Shakes Versus Shav; *Uncollected Works Including* Passion Play; The Cassone; The Gadfly; and Why She Would Not; *Index to the Entire Edition*. London: Bodley Head.

Shershow, Scott Cutler (2001). 'Shakespeare Beyond Shakespeare', *Marxist Shakespeares*, ed. Jean E. Howard and Scott Cutler Shershow. Accents on Shakespeare. London: Routledge, 245–64.

Sidney, Sir Philip (1965). *An Apology for Poetry: Or The Defence of Poesy*, ed. Geoffrey Shepherd. London: Nelson.

Simpson, J. A., and Weiner, E. S. C. (eds.) (1989). *The Oxford English Dictionary*. Vol. 1: A–Bazouki. Oxford: Clarendon Press.

Sokol, B. J. (1994). 'The Problem of Assessing Thomas Harriot's *A Briefe and True Report of His Discoveries in North America*'. *Annals of Science* 51: 1–16.

——— and Sokol, Mary (2000). *Shakespeare's Legal Language: A Dictionary*. London: Athlone.

Spencer, Terence (1953). 'Shakespeare Learns the Value of Money: The Dramatist at Work on *Timon of Athens*'. *Shakespeare Survey* 6: 75–8.

Spurgeon, Caroline (1935). *Shakespeare's Imagery and What it Tells Us*. Cambridge: Cambridge University Press.

Stalin, Joseph (1941). *Dialectical and Historical Materialism*. London: Lawrence and Wishart.

Stallybrass, Peter (1998). 'Marx's Coat', *Border Fetishisms: Material Objects in Unstable Spaces*, ed. Patricia Spyer. New York: Routledge, 183–207.

Stone, Lawrence (1965). *The Crisis of the Aristocracy 1558–1641*. Oxford: Clarendon.

Stubbes, Philip (2002). *The Anatomie of Abuses*, ed. Margaret Jane Kidnie. Tempe, Ariz.: Renaissance English Text Society.

Swift, Jonathan (1985). *Gulliver's Travels*, ed. Peter Dixon and John Chalker. Introd. Michael Foot. London: Penguin.

Taylor, Gary (1983). '*King Lear*: The Date and Authorship of the Folio Version', *The Division of the Kingdoms: Shakespeare's Two Versions of* King Lear, ed. Gary Taylor and Michael Warren. Oxford: Clarendon, 351–468.

——— and Warren, Michael (eds.) (1983). *The Division of the Kingdoms: Shakespeare's Two Versions of* King Lear. Oxford: Clarendon Press.

Thompson, E. P. (1963). *The Making of the English Working Class*. London: Victor Gollancz.

Tillotson, Geoffrey (1945). 'Review of E. M. W. Tillyard *Shakespeare's History Plays* (London: Chatto and Windus, 1944)'. *English* 5: 160–1.

Tillyard, E. M. W. (1943). *The Elizabethan World Picture*. London: Chatto and Windus.

——— (1944). *Shakespeare's History Plays*. London: Chatto and Windus.

Warburton, William (1741). *The Divine Legation of Moses*. Vol. 2. London: Fletcher Gyles.

Wayne, Valerie (1991). 'Introduction', *The Matter of Difference: Materialist Feminist Criticism of Shakespeare*, ed. Valerie Wayne. Ithaca, N.Y.: Cornell University Press, 1–26.

Weeks, John (1981). *Capital and Exploitation*. London: Edward Arnold.

Weimann, Robert (1978). *Shakespeare and the Popular Tradition in the Theatre: Studies in the Social Dimension of Dramatic Form and Function*, ed. Robert Schwartz. Baltimore, Md.: Johns Hopkins University Press.

—— (1988). 'Bifold Authority in Shakespeare's Theatre'. *Shakespeare Quarterly* 39: 401–17.

Wells, Robin Headlam (1985). 'The Fortunes of Tillyard: Twentieth-century Critical Debate on Shakespeare's History Plays'. *English Studies* 66: 391–403.

—— (2000). ' "Manhood and Chevalrie": *Coriolanus*, Prince Henry, and the Chivalric Revival'. *Review of English Studies* 51: 395–422.

Wells, Stanley, Taylor, Gary, Jowett, John, and Montgomery, William (1987). *William Shakespeare: A Textual Companion*. Oxford: Oxford University Press.

West, Alick (1937). *Crisis and Criticism*. London: Lawrence and Wishart.

Wiggins, Martin (2000). *Shakespeare and the Drama of His Time*. Oxford: Oxford University Press.

Wilcher, Robert (1997). 'Double Endings and Autonomous Acts: A Feature of Shakespearian Design'. *Cahiers Élisabéthains* 51: 47–61.

Williams, Penry (1995). *The Later Tudors: England 1547–1603*. Oxford: Clarendon Press.

Williams, Raymond (1958). *Culture and Society, 1780–1950*. London: Chatto and Windus.

—— (1973). *The Country and the City*. London: Chatto and Windus.

—— (1977). *Marxism and Literature*. Oxford: Oxford University Press.

—— (1985). 'Afterword', *Political Shakespeare: New Essays in Cultural Materialism*, ed. Jonathan Dollimore and Alan Sinfield. Manchester: Manchester University Press, 231–9.

Wilson, John Dover (1935). *What Happens in* Hamlet. Cambridge: Cambridge University Press.

Wilson, Richard (2001). 'The Management of Mirth: Shakespeare Via Bourdieu', *Marxist Shakespeares*, ed. Jean E. Howard and Scott Cutler Shershow. London: Routledge, 159–77.

Wimsatt, W. K., and Beardsley, M. C. (1946). 'The Intentional Fallacy'. *Sewanee Review* 54: 468–88.

Winsten, Stephen (1951). *Days with Bernard Shaw*. London: Hutchinson.

Index